Know your Coffee.

An illustrated guide to coffee culture

By Stevie Wilson
Edited by Vita Ayala

Second printing 2013

http://coffee.genkiinc.net

http://genkiinc.net

swinku.tumblr.com

sw.inku@gmail.com

Coffee Culture

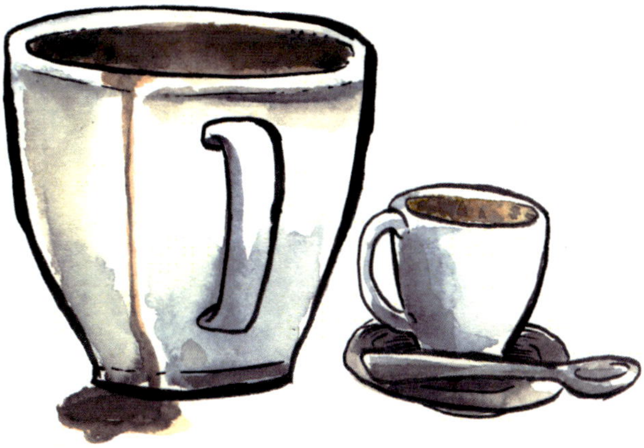

Coffee has gone from being something incredibly simple in this country, to something that is complex and even confounding at times. It has been rebranded as a whole and become something of a trend. With the rise of coffeehouse chains that are popping up on every corner has come the rise of what can be referred to as **coffee culture**. All across America people can order drinks that are so far removed from the original idea of brewed coffee that some would hardly consider these drinks coffee at all. There is a clear divide that has emerged because of this: the "*coffee snob*" versus the "*candy coffee drinkers*", with hardly any communication in between the camps.

As a **barista** I had drink orders given to me that are so complicated I have had to pause and seriously sort out what on earth they just asked for. Most casual coffee drinkers do not actually know what they are ordering when they order it. Or truly know the difference between good coffee and terrible coffee.

In order to bridge the gap and clear up misinformation, I offer this book as a quick guide to those who enjoy coffee and want to know their drink further. So now, if you let me, I would love to help guide you a little bit into that confusing world of coffee, and to help you answer the question of: ***what on earth did you just order?***

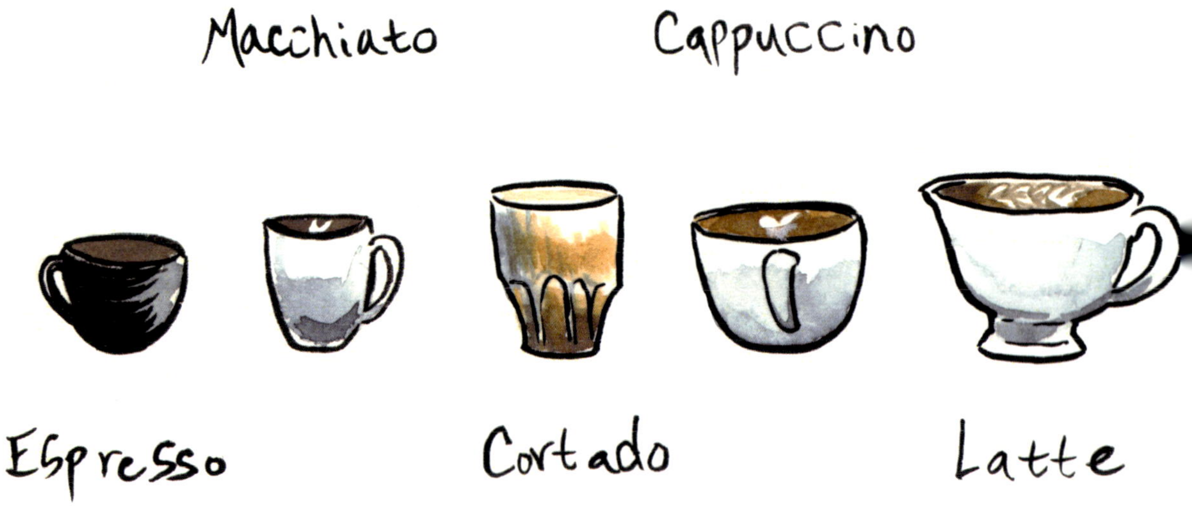
Macchiato
Cappuccino
Espresso
Cortado
Latte

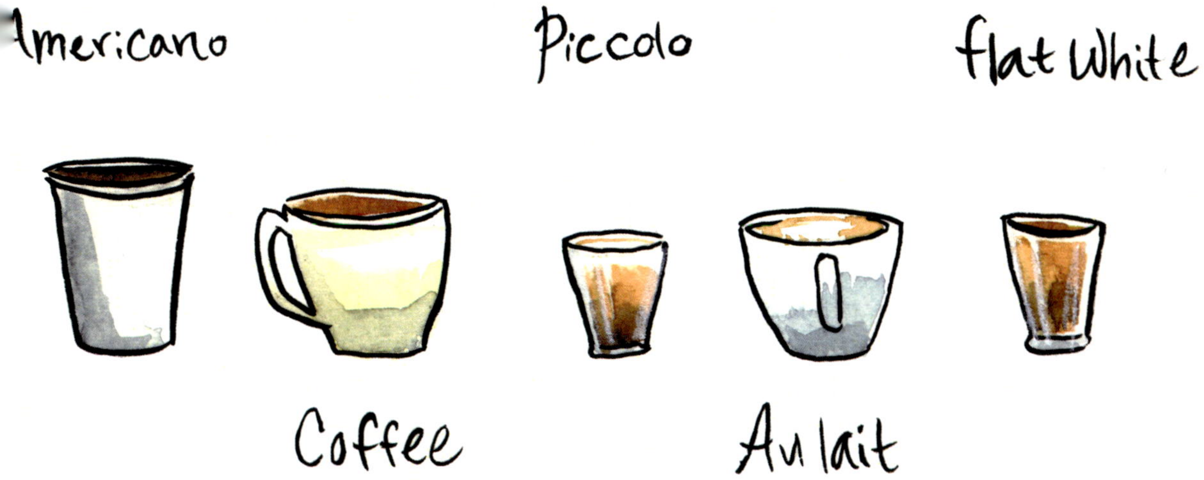
Americano
Piccolo
Flat White
Coffee
Au lait

Life of a bean

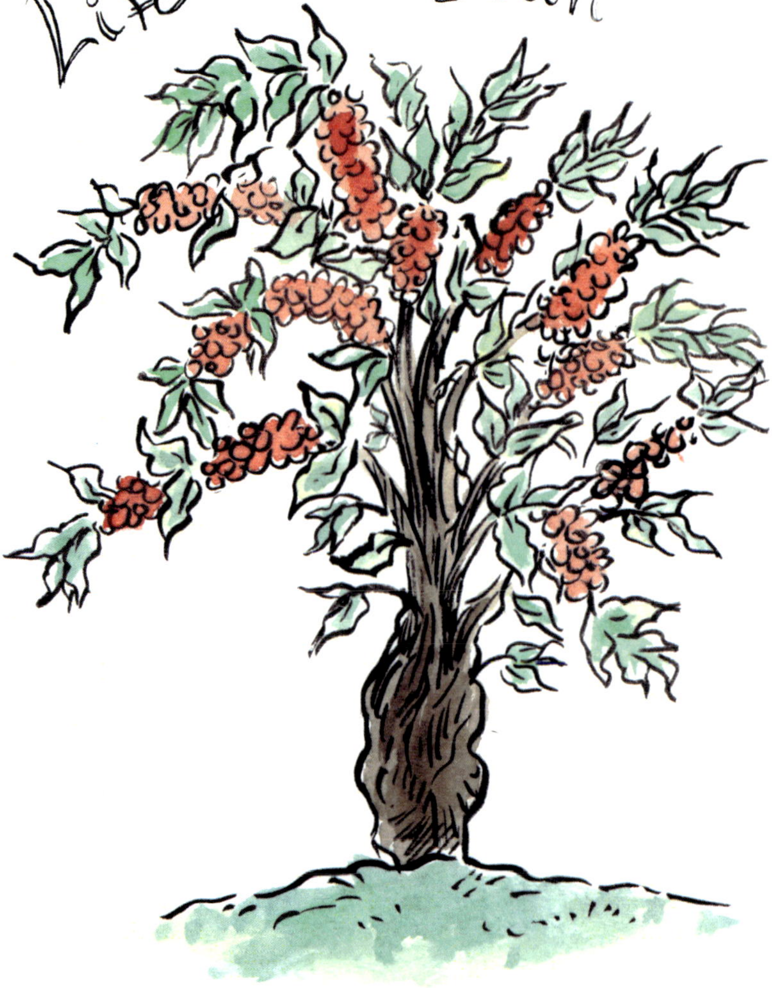

Coffee beans come from a fruit called coffee cherries; they are the pit. The cherry skin and pulp must be removed before the bean can be roasted. There are several different ways to do this.

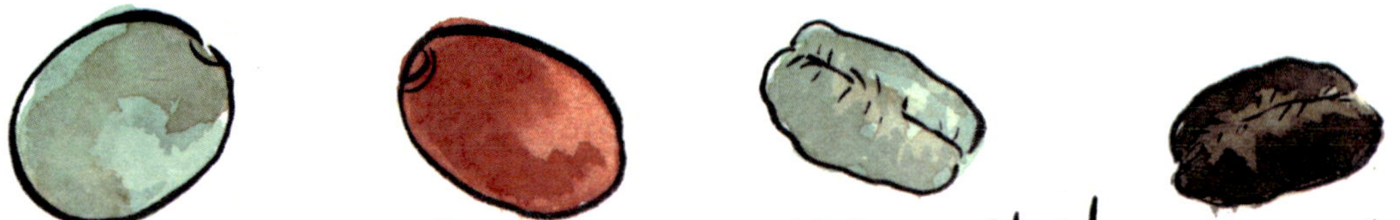

the Main Methods for Processing Coffee Cherries

While coffee comes from all over, warm climate countries are the most supportive. Ultimately, the water source of that country is what helps determine how they will process the cherries.

The **inside** of the coffee cherry is made up of several layers, even before you get to the pit/bean at the center. The process to remove the bean is pretty involved

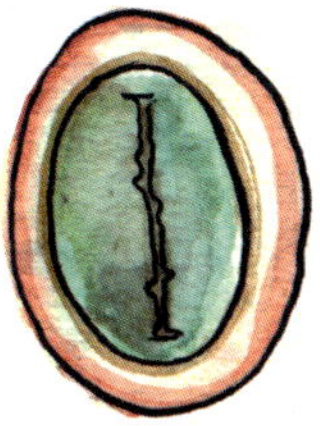

- Skin
- Pulp
- Mucilage
- Parchment
- Silver Skin
- Bean

Wet and **Dry** process each are contributing factors to what flavor notes occur in the beans.

Wet Process

After the cherries are picked, the skins and fruit are removed using water. The coffee cherries are immersed in water, the bad or unripe cherries float to the top, while the good ones sink. The fruit is machine pressed through a screen to help remove so of the pulp and skin.

After the first round, the coffee cherries will have to be processed again with a ferment-and-wash method or some form of mechanical de-mucilaging. (removal of leftover skin and pulp.)

The beans are then machine or sun dried, after which they have to be shelled to remove the parchment and silver skin encasing the bean. Only then are the beans ready for roasting.

Dry process

This is the oldest way of preparing coffee beans for roasting. The coffee cherries are washed and laid out to dry in the sun, after the bad and damaged cherries are sorted out by water or machine. While drying, the cherries must be rotated and raked to ensure even drying out, or they will mildew. It can take up to 4 weeks for the cherries to dry to optimal moisture levels; the weather and humidity can affect this. If dried to long the beans will can become brittle.

Once the beans are ready for hulling*, they are sent to a mill to be hulled sorted, graded, and bagged. They are then ready for roasting.

*Hulling is like shelling for coffee beans, its when you remove the dried left over skin around the bean.

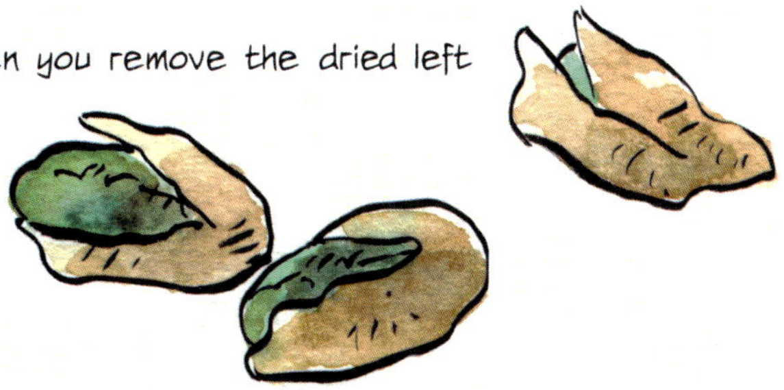

The yield, quality, and process, as well as certifications, attribute to the cost of the beans on the coffee market.

Coffee regions

The main ones you see on market.

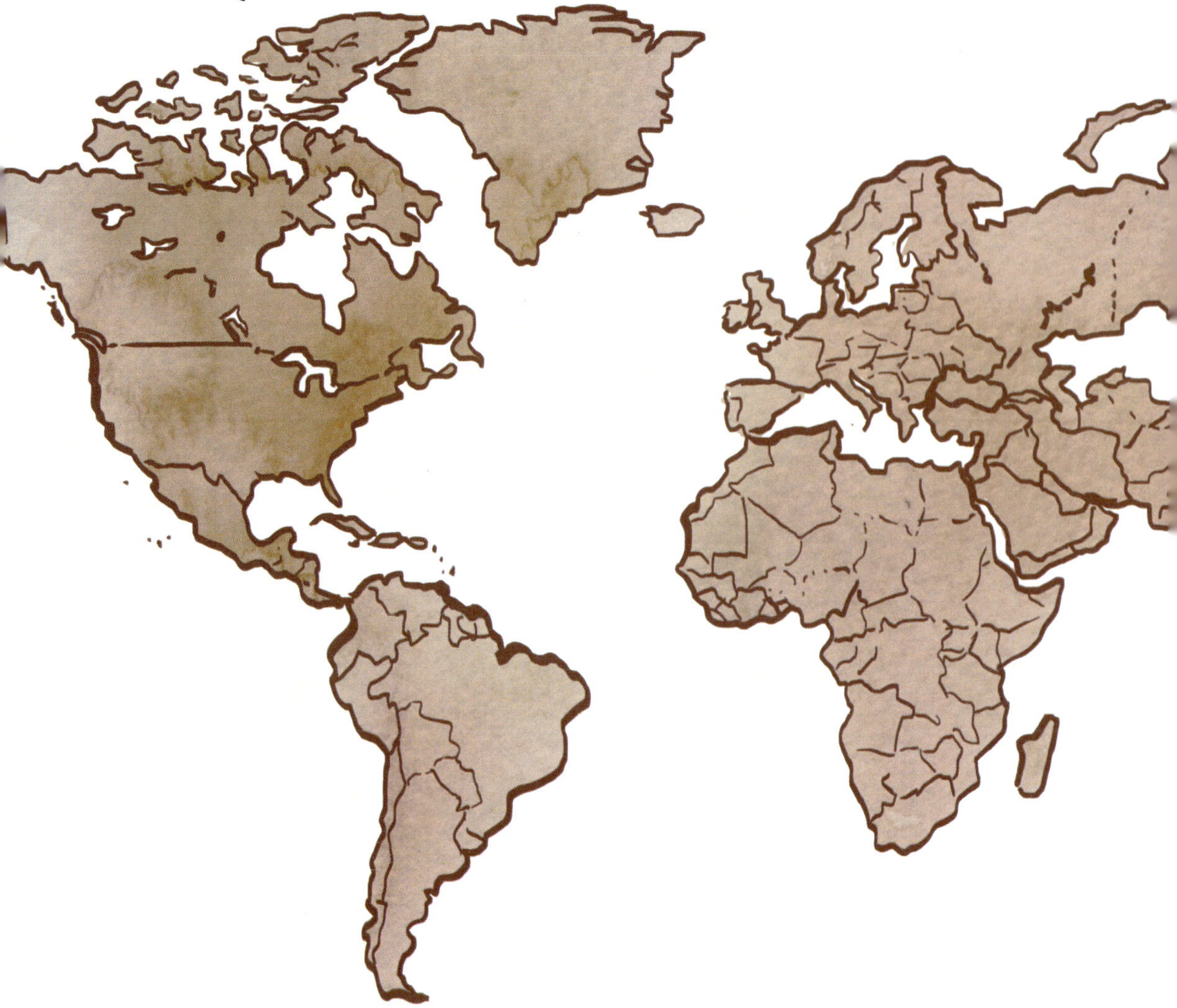

Africa & Arabia: Burundi, Congo, Ethiopia, Kenya, Rwanda, Tanzania, Uganda, Yemen, Zambia, and Zimbabwe.

Most of these countries use the Dry process because of limited water, and it gives the beans a distinct, strong flavor profile, often with citrus or bright in flavor.

The Americas: Brasil, Colombia, Costa Rica, El Salvador, Ecuador, Guatemala, Honduras, Mexico, Nicaragua, and Panama.
Most are rainforest climate grown. They are considered medium roasts, are often used in breakfast blends, and are smooth, mild, and balanced in flavor.

Asia/Indonesia/The Pacific: Bali, India, Java, New Guinea, Sulawesi, and Sumatra,.
Very varied in flavor, sumatra coffee is famous for being dark and earthy. While New Guinea beans are sweet and dessert like in flavor profile.

Islands: Australia, The Dominican Republic, Hawaii (certified Kona), Jamaica (certified Blue Mountain) and Puerto Rico.

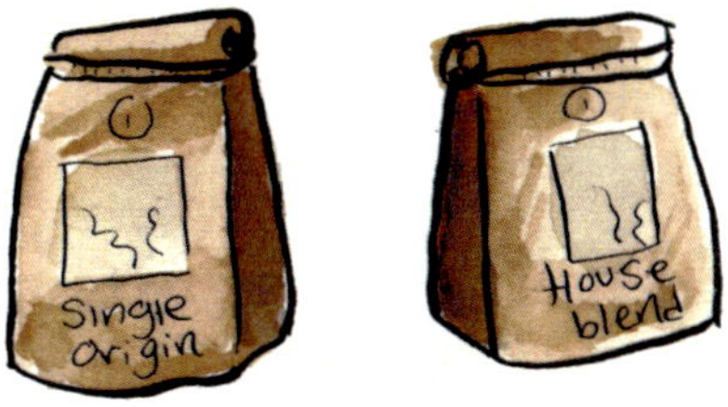

Origins Vs. Blends

"Single Origin"

Beans that come from a **single** farm or region.
There is a lot of debate if this can apply only to a single farm, or if in the case of multiple cooperatives if they can qualify as a single origin because they share a region.

"Blends"

Coffee blends are mixed regions selected and sold by Roasters.
Blends that are sold under a non-region name like a "house blend" are made up of a selection of beans from different regions that are mixed together to complement each other. Most cafe's serve two blends, one for drip coffee and one for espresso, to give some consistency to the coffee they serve month to month.

House blends usually rotate their bean selection based on what is available on the market. If you notice your coffee blend seems different this is why. Blends always list what was used to make them. Most espressos are blends, not just a single bean roast, to get an optimal flavor profile for being drank as a shot.

Certifications are proof of certain criteria being met by the coffee farms and roasters, most of them are for certain environmental safety standards. You can find these listed on each bag of coffee.

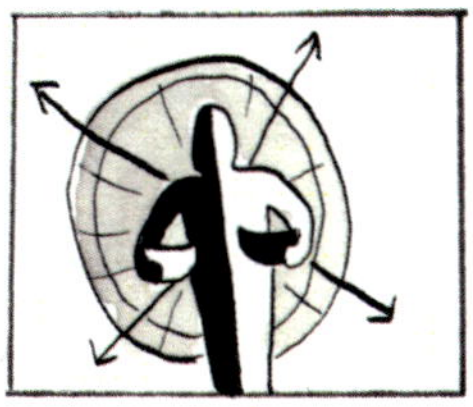

← ***Fair trade label***

Fair trade certification: Commonly seen on "single origin" coffees; certifying the coffee was harvested from democratically-organized cooperatives of small producers, not individually-owned farms, estates, or farms that use hired labor.

Other certifications:

USD - Meets U.S.A standards for organicly grown.
Bird friendly - Shade grown, so trees in the surrounding area arent cut down.
Rainforest alliance - Certfied sustainability grown coffee.
UTZ - Farms show complience for good agricultural practices, habitat protection buisness transparency and traceability.

Whats the difference

Same beans

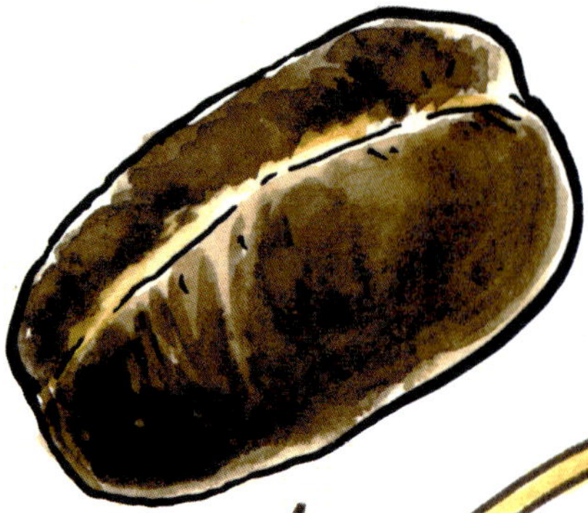

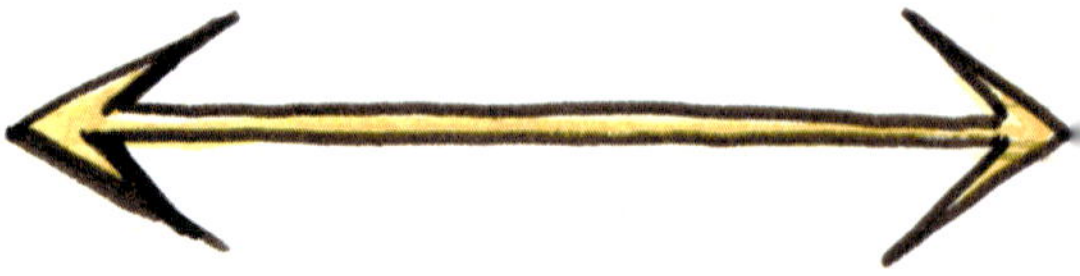

Dark to medium roast

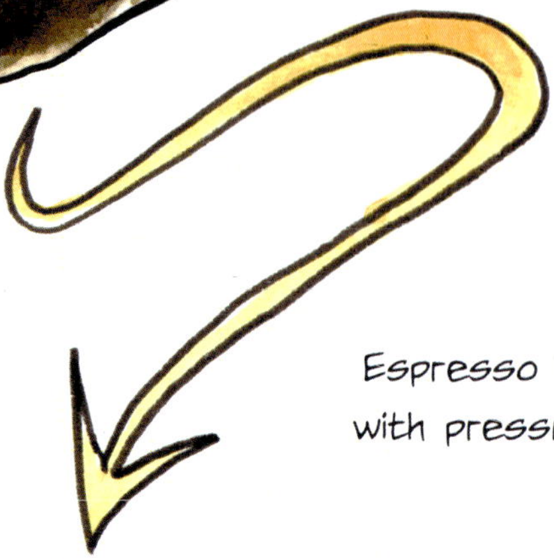

Espresso is ***fine ground beans,*** extracted with pressurized hot water in and served in ***2oz shots.***

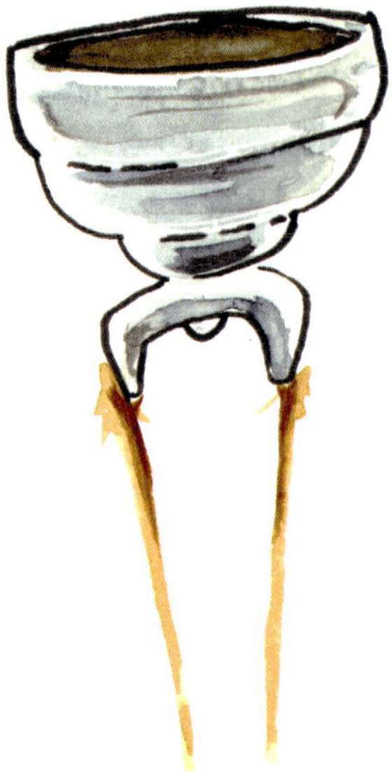

Espresso beans are selected by how well they taste when finely extracted.

Beans with chocolaty ***flavor notes*** tend to be better for espresso then citrusy or earthy tasting coffee beans.

Espresso beans must sit for a week after roasting, before they can be used. Because all beans release gases, if the beans are used too soon, the espresso will have air bubbles. This is why coffee bags have a one way vent so the bags don't ***explode***.

between Espresso & Coffee?

different roasts.

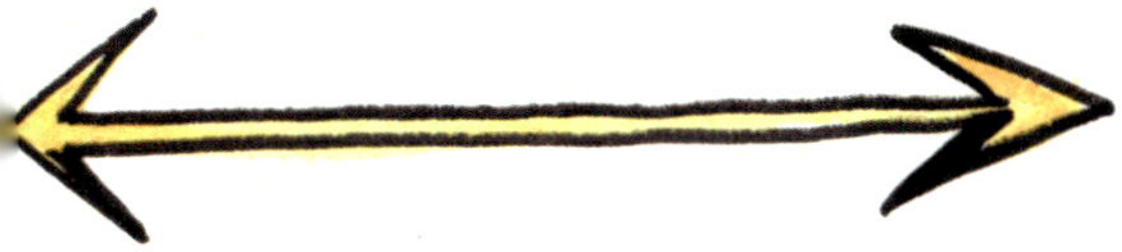

medium to light roast

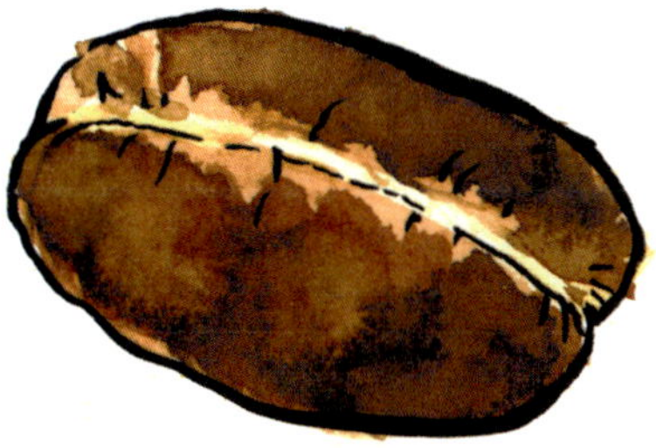

Drip coffee is medium to coarse ground beans, brewed by hot water through a filter. Either by automatic coffee makers or pour over. It is served in cups 8oz-24oz

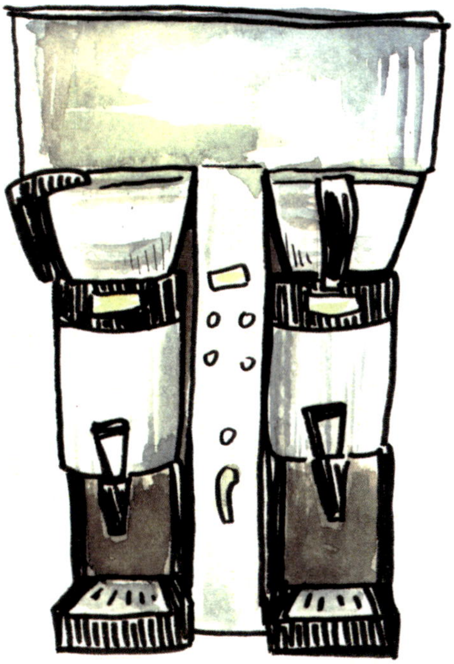

Because so much water is present in drip coffee any beans can be used for it, the flavors are less in your face then espresso since its diluted.

You ***can*** use espresso beans for drip coffee or drip beans for espresso, but they may not make as good tasting a drink.

Espresso

The base of most coffee drinks. It is finely ground, concentrated coffee that is extracted using pressure & hot water. It's mostly bean oil, and is thick in consistency.

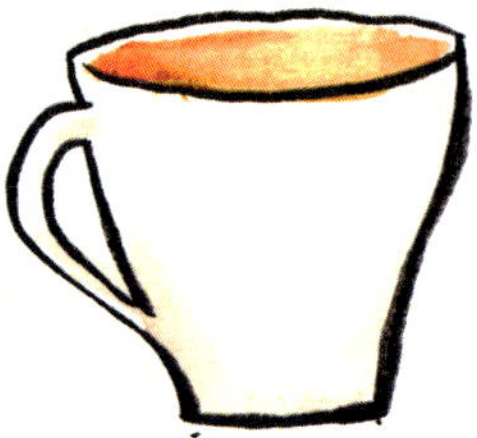

2oz

It embodies both the best & worst qualities in coffee, having both a full body and a sharp bitterness to it, but also an underlying sweetness.

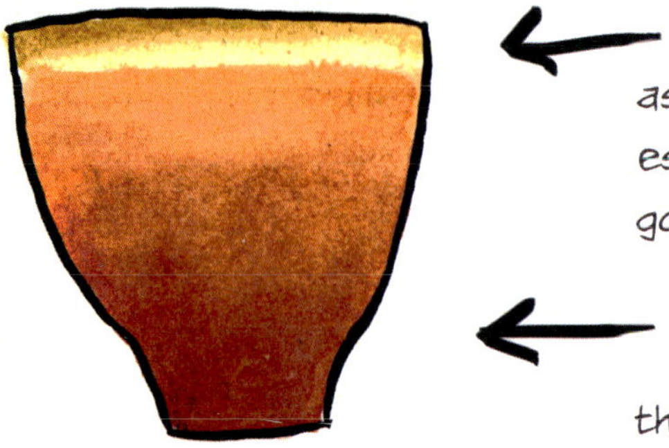

Crema

as the shot ***finishes***, the espresso thins and forms a golden foam.

Body

the strong flavor that comes from the ***beginning*** of the shot

"How can you tell if its a good shot?"

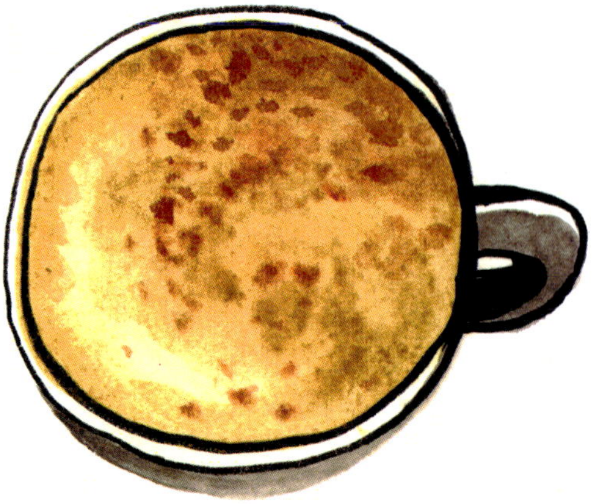

Espresso is a traditional Italian drink. It takes time to build a palette for drinking it by its self.

Good espresso shots start strong but have a clean, sweet finish that don't taste lemony or sour.

Visually on a good shot you can see flaking or "leopard spots" on the surface of the crema.

The difference between a **single** and a **double** shot is the amount of grams of espresso the basket holds

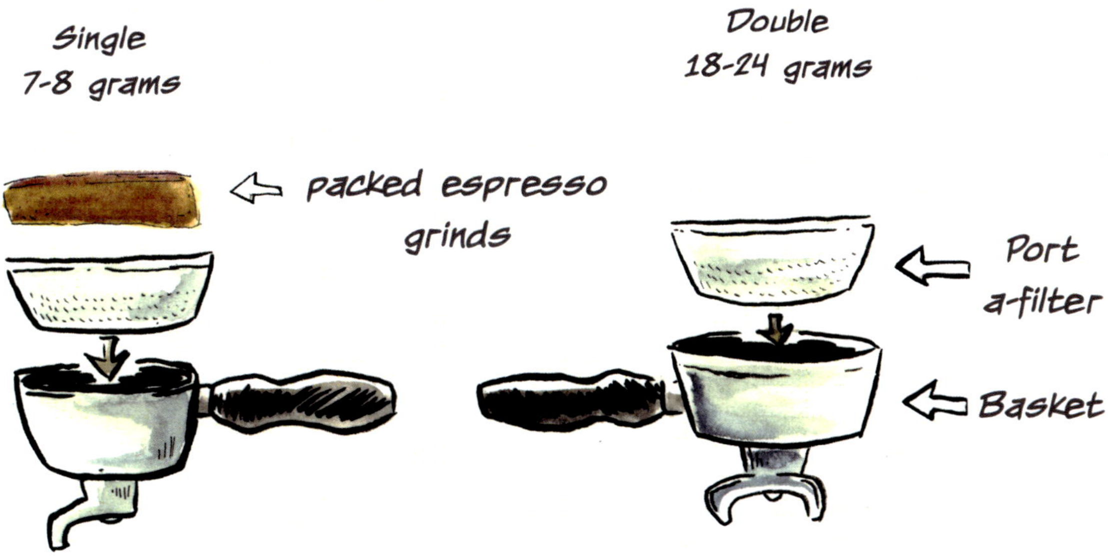

Running describes the rate of extraction.

A shot should extract within **25-30** seconds. And should flow out a smooth steady pace in a fine stream.

Pulling → the term for **running** a shot. Espresso machines used to have levers, do you had to ***"pull"***.

Short shot (aka Ristretto) → **ending** the shot before the espresso runs a **complete shot**. This makes it so it's a stronger and more bitter espresso shot.

Long shot → an **over pulled** shot that is more watery and weak flavored.

The barista controls the length of the shot as well as amount of espresso packed in the basket, which is why having a well trained skilled barista is a major part in good coffee. ***(Tip your barista!)***

Burr grinder

Also known as a **step grinder** or an **espresso grinder.**

These grinders are used only for grinding beans for ***espresso***; baristas use them to make espresso to order. The barista controls the amount of espresso that is ground. The grounds should be used within 5 minutes of grinding, because air exposure causes clumping and ruins the consistency.

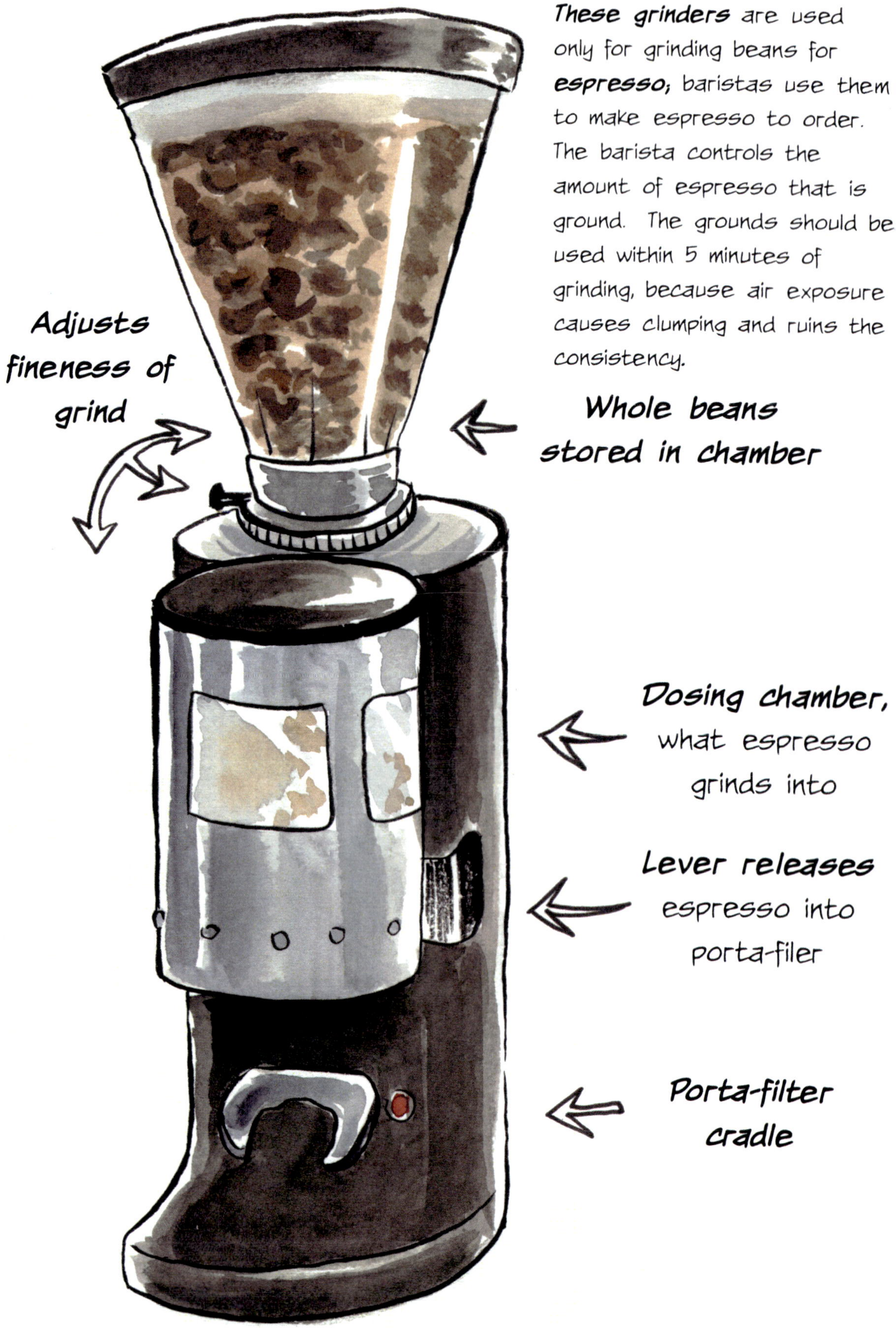

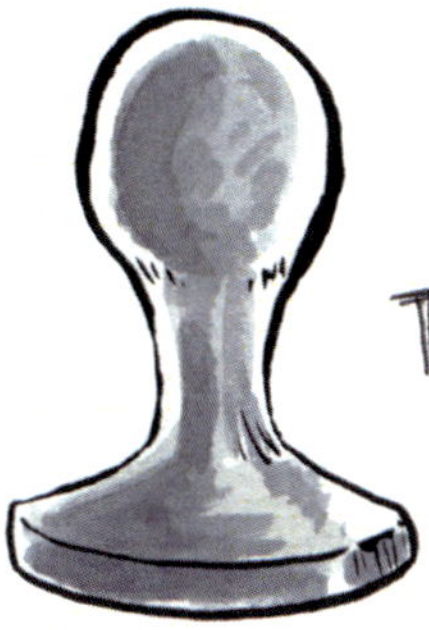

Tamper

Espresso has to be packed into its porta-filter before you can pull a shot. It takes about 30lbs of pressure to properly pack espresso, which is exerted by the barista.

The **tamper** has a metal smooth or curved bottom, made to fit snugly into the espresso basket with no room on the sides.

Tamping It is a multi-stepped process.

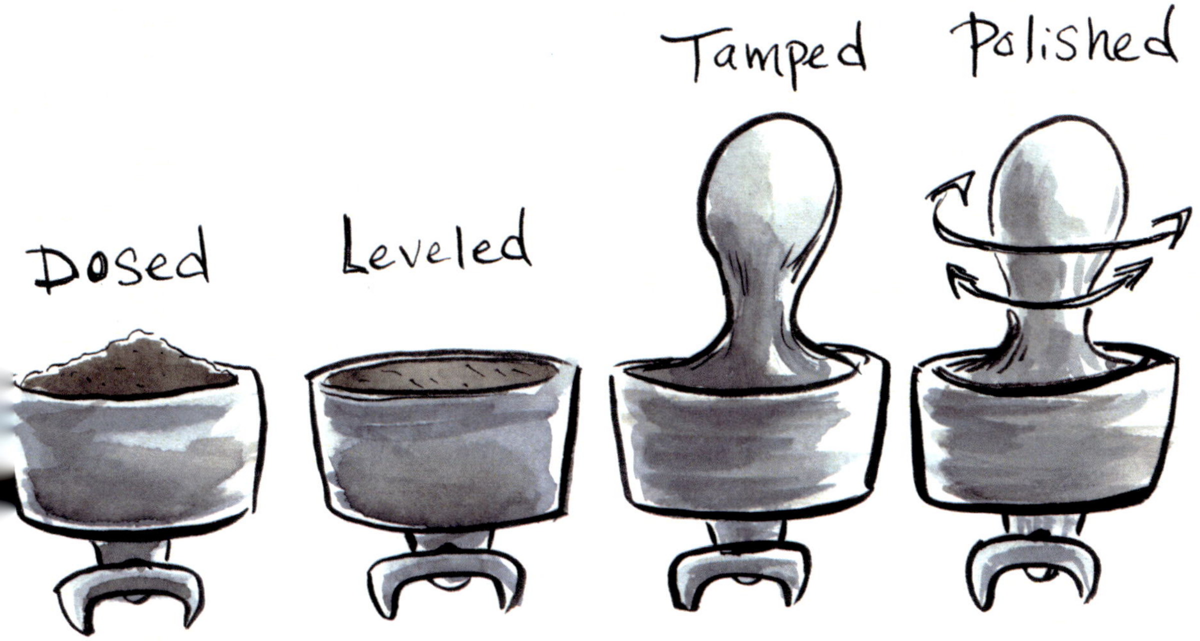

Loose ground espresso after its been dosed from grinder, **piled** in a slight mound

Fingers are used to **level** or **pat down** grounds into basket before "tamping"

Tamper is used to **pack down** espresso into basket

Tamper is **gently spun** in basket with no pressure to smooth puck surface

Don't knock it!

Knocking is a technique used by some baristas to knock excessive espresso from the sides of the basket before the shot is run. This is done by tapping the side of the basket with the tamper, or by giving the whole porta-filter a hard tap on the counter. It's been argued that this forms cracks in the espresso puck and gives water weaker areas to flow through, which degrades the shot.

Cappuccino

There are two different "**styles**" of cappuccinos:

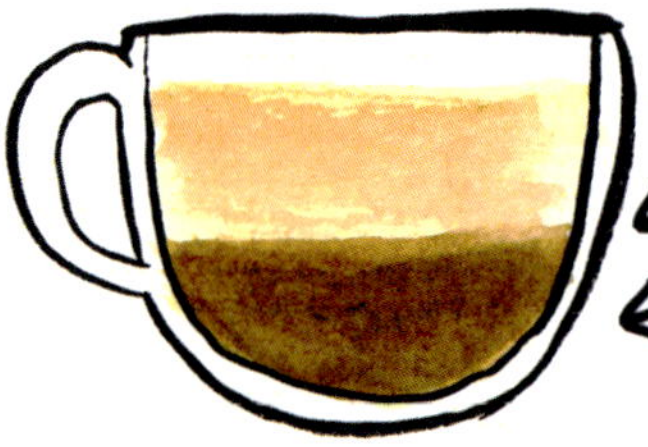

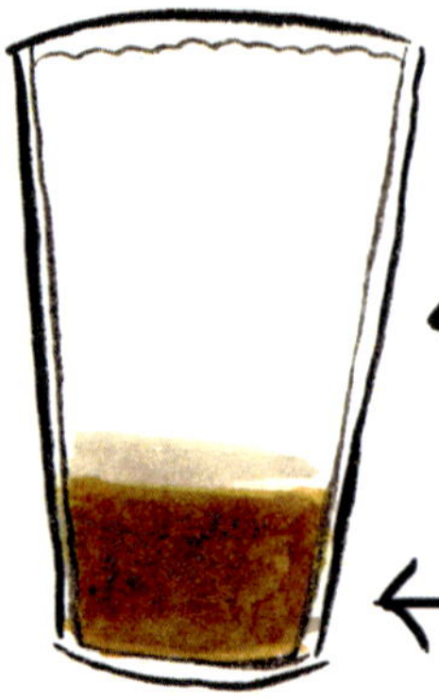

True **wet style** cappuccinos are only meant to be **6oz-8oz** in size. The foam in this version is called micro foam and is slightly thicker then latte milk, though is still very smooth compared to the all foam cappuccino.

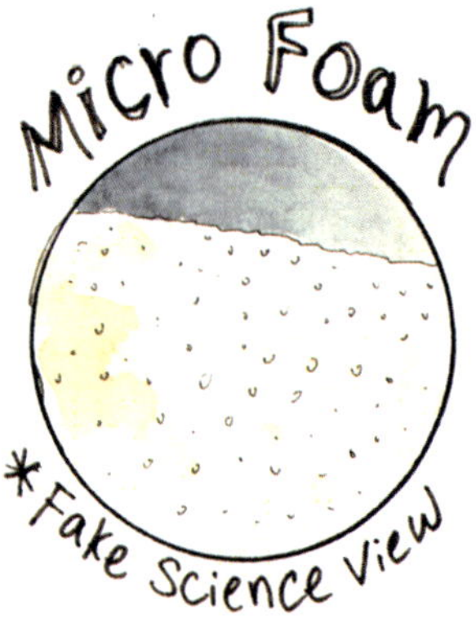

Micro foam is made up of very tiny air bubbles and is created by raising the milk temperature and adding just enough air to the surface.

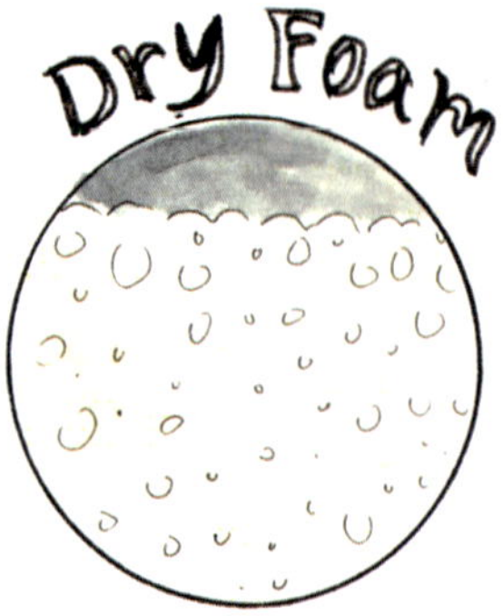

The **American** dry cappuccino has what is called 'dry foam.' Dry foam is created when the milk is steamed to form a "meringue" like milk that causes the water in the milk to separate from their proteins.

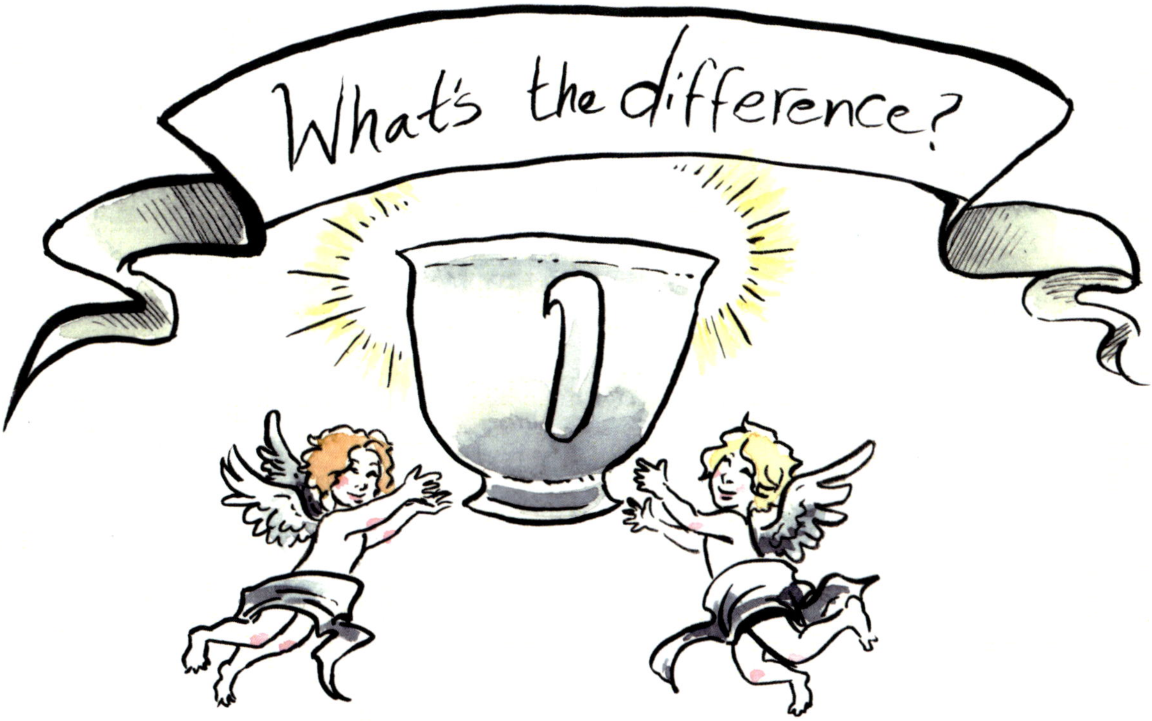

Wet cappuccinos are heated to 140 degrees F, which is the ***"just too hot to touch"*** temperature. That temperature allows the cappuccino to be perfect to drink without burning your mouth, and there is a natural sweetness to the milk that compliments the espresso. A good wet cappuccino has very little bitterness and can be drunk without any sugar.

To achieve the dry foam you have to ***overheat*** the milk past optimal temperatures.

Extra hot milk losses this sweetness because of the separation of the proteins and water from the milk, and becomes dry and less flavorful as well, as scalding.

Fact: Traditionally in Italy cappuccino's were meant to be a breakfast only drink, and wouldn not be drunk after lunch.

Latte

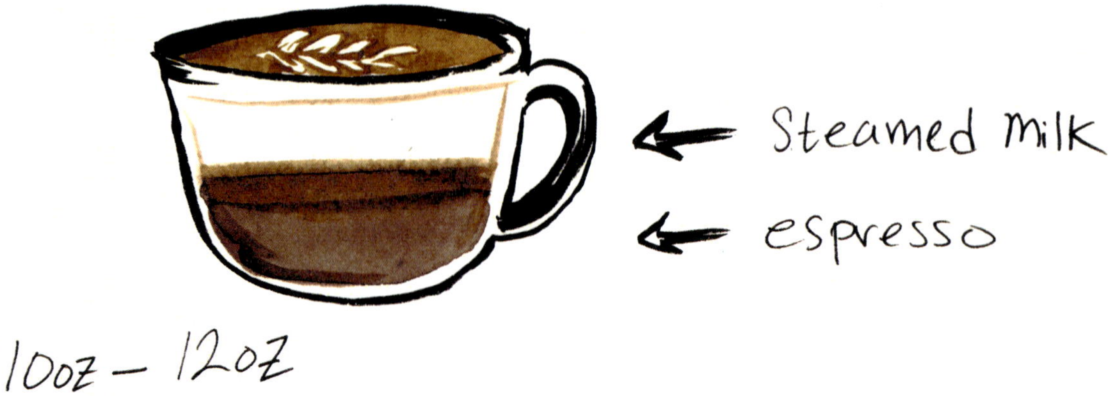

Actually the real name is "***Cafe Latte***", Latte just means "milk" but most people just call it a Latte in America.

A ***good*** latte has a very thin foam with no notable bubbles. And the milk in a latte should not be scalding hot; you shouldn't have to wait to drink it.

Lattes have ***more milk*** because of their size, and the silky consistency allows for more detailed and delicate milk art than its cappuccino counterpart.

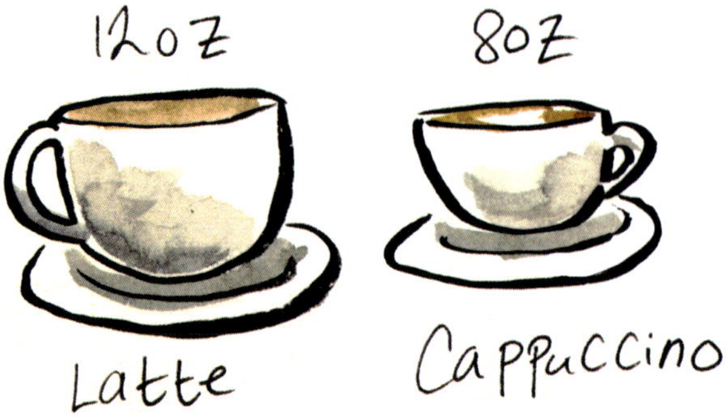

Latte Art

Milk art is a skill learned by baristas that requires good espresso, good milk steaming, and **a lot of practice.**

Pourart

Is **pouring** the milk into shapes, on the surface of espresso. It's achieved with wrist movement, pour speed and the direction of the stream of milk.

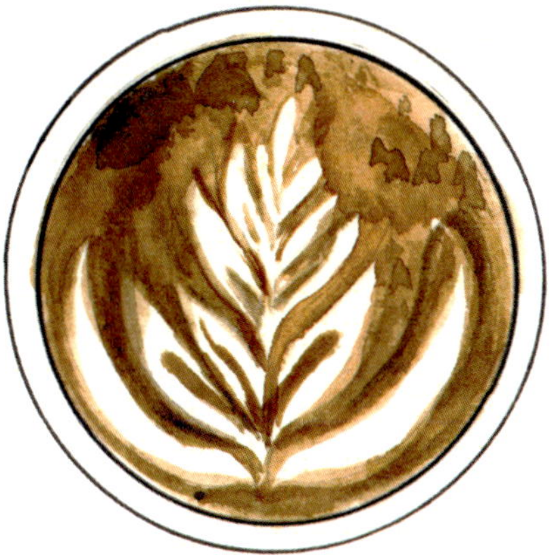

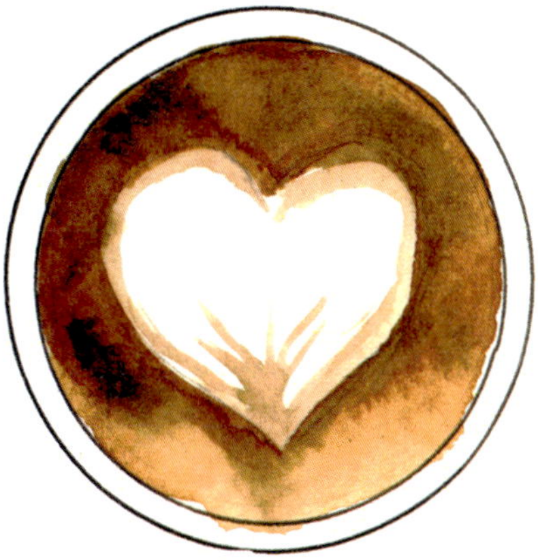

Technically **rosettes** are only supposed to be for lattes. Because the **slightly thicker** cappuccino foam doesn't hold detail as well.

Etching

Etching is when you drag toothpicks or stir sticks through the foam to make designs you can't get by pouring.

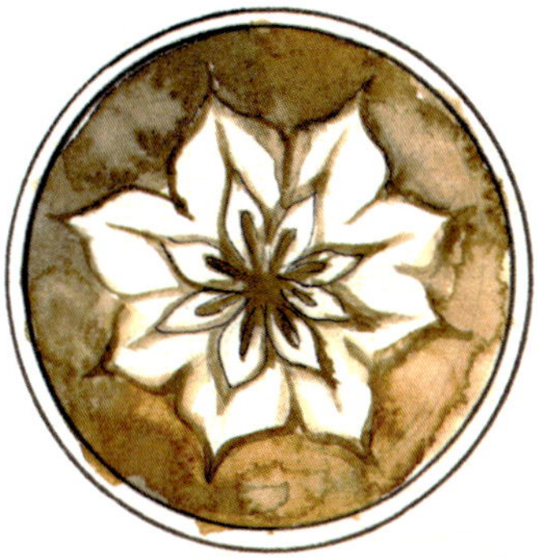

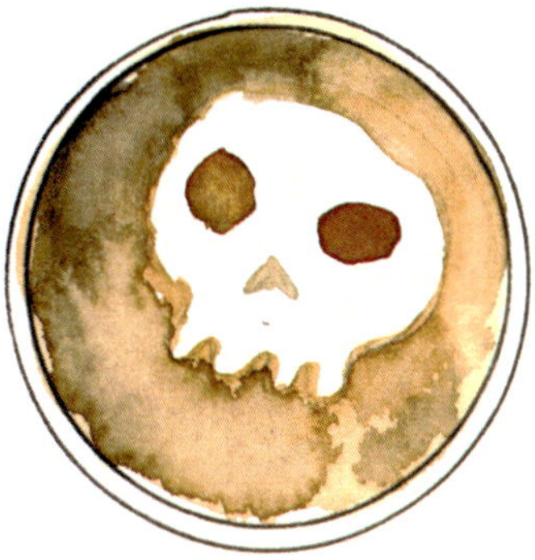

The basics of pouring

Pouring is a ***3 step process*** that takes place after the milk is steamed. It's a technique used to pour designs in Lattes and other steamed milk drinks. Three important factors in the art of pouring are milk quality, pour speeds and control.

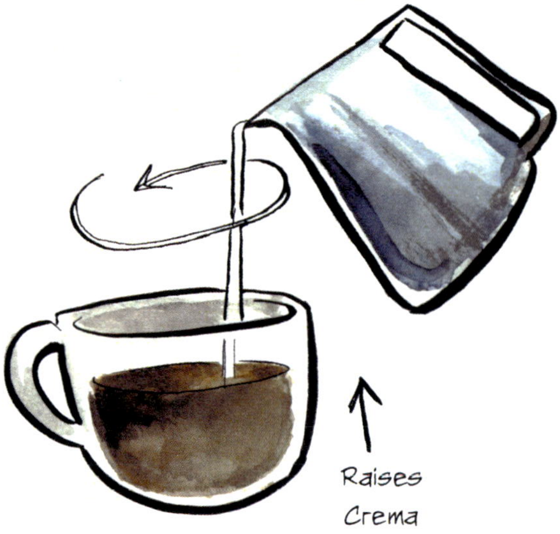

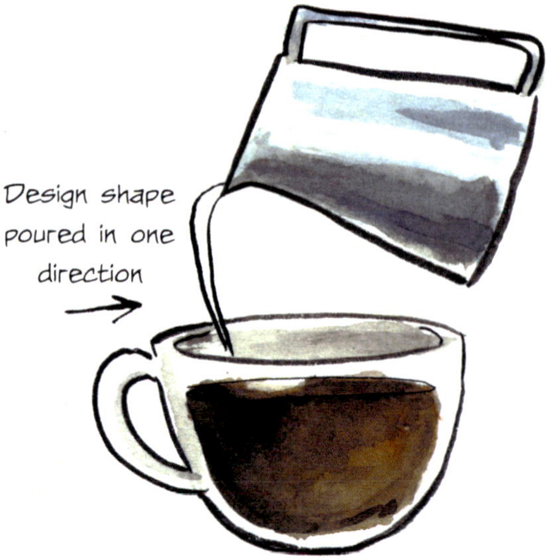

① Slow pour

Milk pitcher is tilted slightly to pour a slow steady stream of milk in a gentle circular motion around cup. This is done until the cup is half full. This method is used to introduce milk into the espresso, but also keep the crema surface, because it helps hold the design shape.

② Medium pour

After the cup is half full, the milk is poured a little faster and the first half of the design is poured.
EX. zig zags for ferns, circles for hearts and tulips.

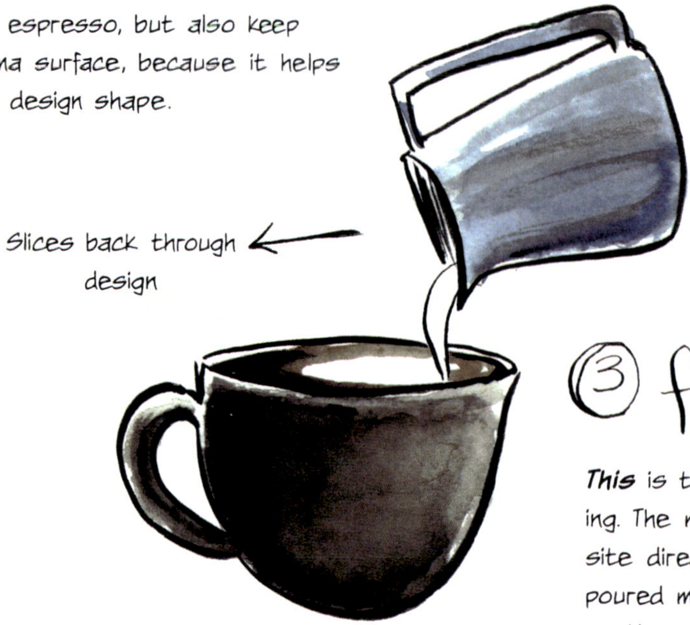

③ fast pour

This is the finishing stage of pouring. The milk is poured in the opposite direction back over the already poured milk which should be visible on the espresso surface. The milk is dragged back, and it splits the design, creating the finished look. It is ***important*** not to spill or overfill the cup.

How the design Works

A look at what happens **between** step 2 and 3 of the milk pouring.

① design line is poured in one direction

This varies based on what design is poured. You can achieve multiple designs from slight variation of the pour.

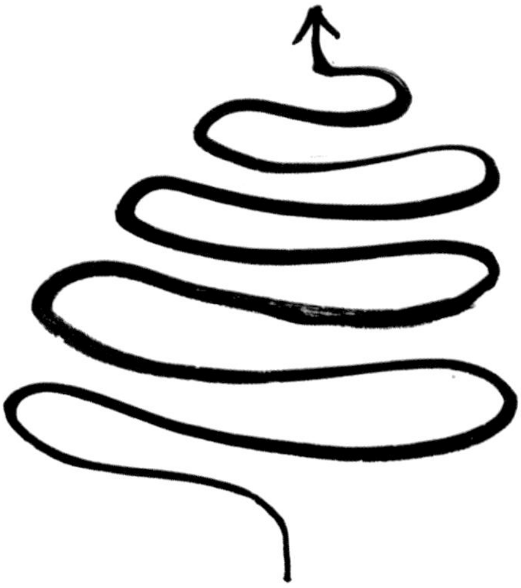

② Reverse pour

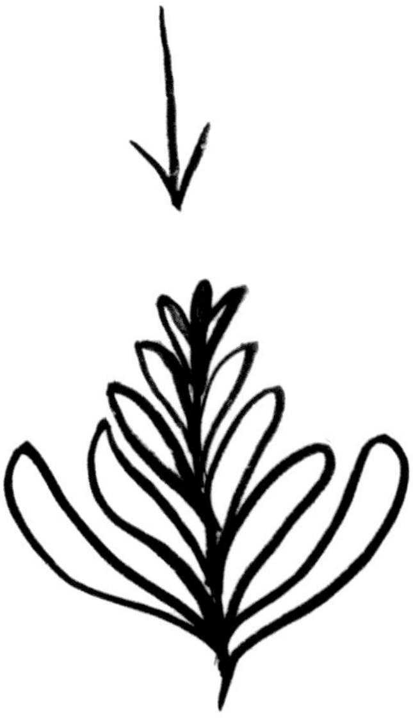

The milk drags a ***line*** down the ***middle of the design*** and creates and image. Sort of like a Rorschach test, this pulling effect can also be achieved by dragging a toothpick through the foam which is how "etching" designs work.

Fact: Some baristas and cafe's compete in "Throw down" pouring competitions. Here, judges grade them by the skill and execution of the pour designs.

Milk Steaming (it's Science)

Steamed milk is more than just hot milk. Boiling milk or microwave it to make "fancy" drinks at home, not the same. Steamed milk is made by introducing a controlled pressurized flow of hot air into cold milk. The process not only adds heat, but it also introduces air to make the foam. Which happens in a matter of seconds - is done in two parts, and is one of the hardest things to learn as a barista. It takes ***a lot*** of practice to get right, and even more to make pretty "drink art" with the foam.

The ***quality*** and ***consistency*** of the foam on steamed milk dictates the difference between types of drinks. Micro foam is the smooth, velvety foam that is the ideal of good drinks. (*See Cappuccinos for more on this*)

Over foaming results in uglier drinks that aren't as tasty, and can be the result of too much surfing, or making the milk to hot.

Surfing

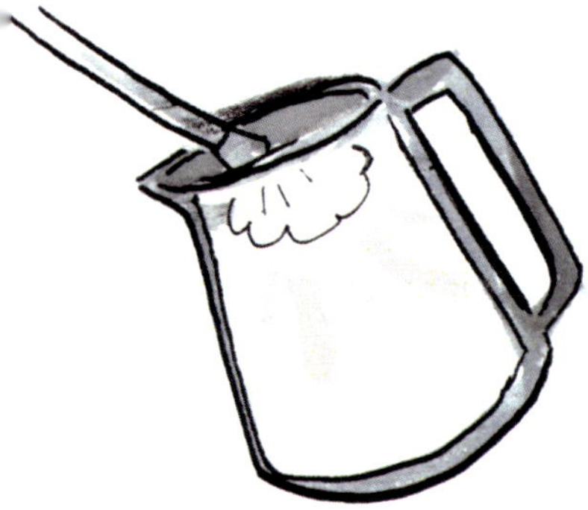

introduces the ***air*** into the milk to thicken it and give it body by creating air bubbles. How long you surf means the difference between a lot of drinks. Lattes and drinks with less foam require a 3 second surf period.

Sinking

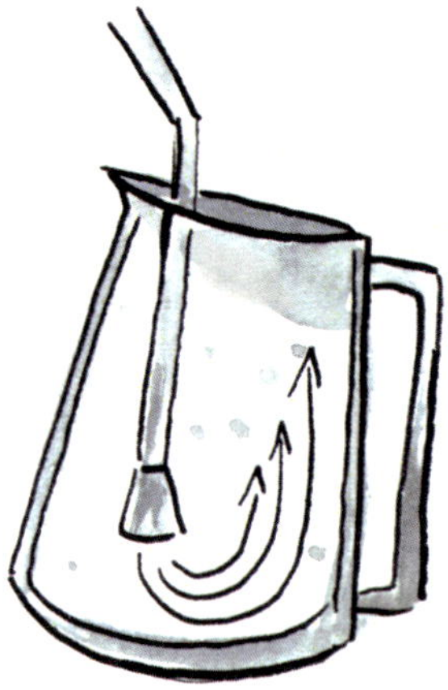

also known as ***stretching*** the milk, is when you sink the steam wand towards the bottom of the pitcher. This is the time in the steaming process your goal is to raise the milk temperature without further aerating. Tilting the pitcher slightly helps create a vortex that cycles the milk smoothly. A thermometer or a hand on the side of the pitcher tells the barista when it's time to cut the air. Depending on the drink, the temperature should be anywhere from 130-140 degrees. Drink, pitchers should be rinsed of milk between uses.

Once the milk has been heated it is no longer milk; the entire compound has changed. The water in the milk breaks and proteins separate. For this reason, it should never be re-steamed.

What is a Macchiato?

Unmentioned coffee chains have caused confusion with their "**caramel macchiato**" aka candy coffee.

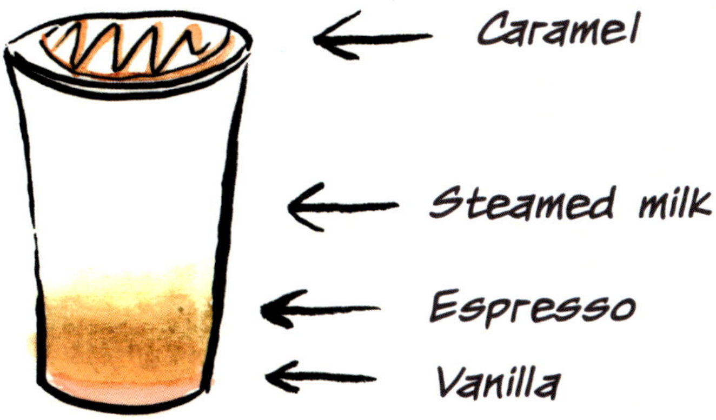

A **real macchiato** is either a shot of espresso with foam, or a shot of espresso with 1 oz of poured steamed milk.

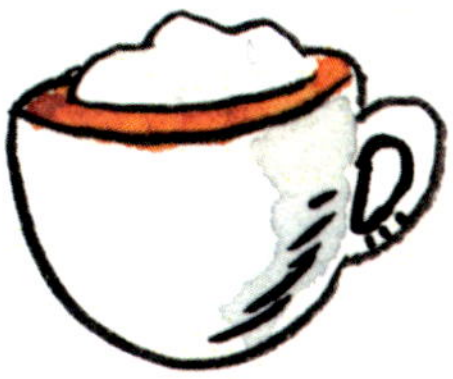

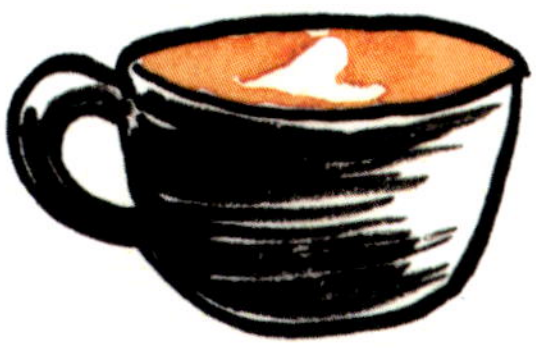

The milk makes it a little smoother than just pure espresso, and it is meant to be drunk in a few sips. Which is why a lot of coffee snobs frown on a "**to go**" Macchiato.

Fact: Most people who order a macchiato know what a real macchiato is, it's a common cafe ordering blunder.

Other Cafe favorites

Mocha

essentially a latte with chocolate.

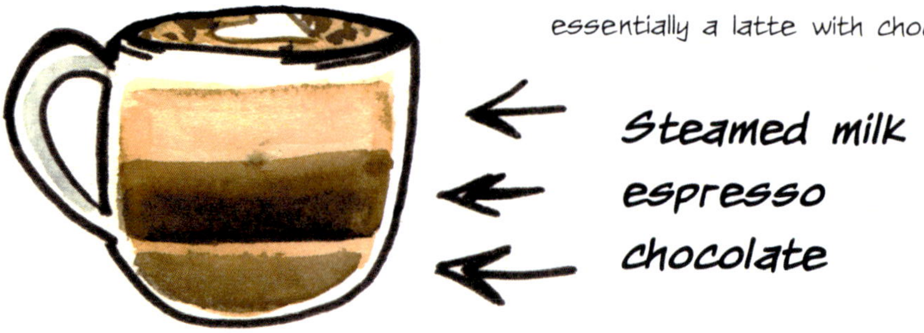

Made with either chocolate syrups, melted down chocolate, chocolate ganache, or hot cocoa mix.

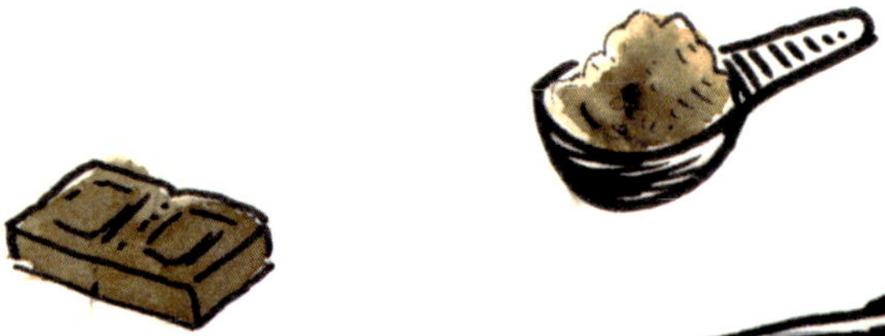

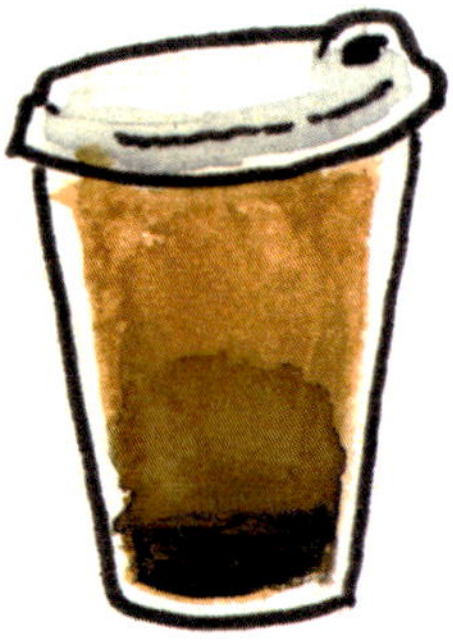

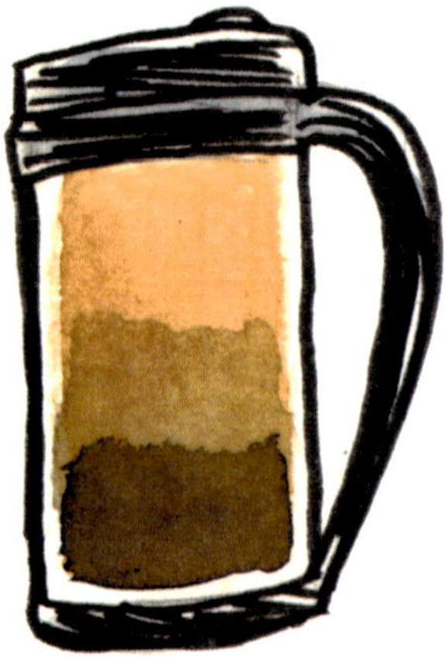

Need more caffeine? Try one of these:

Redeye

a ***single shot*** of epresso added to drip coffee

Blackeye

a ***double shot*** of espresso added to drip coffee.

Americano

The history of the Americano has it that, during WW2 American soldiers stationed in Europe unable to get their customary Joe started getting espresso with hot water added. This drink was dubbed the Americano, which means "**the American**" in Italian.

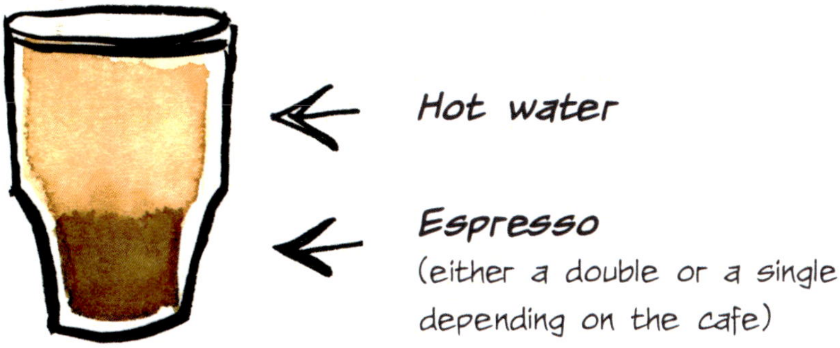

Another variation is called a **"Long black."**

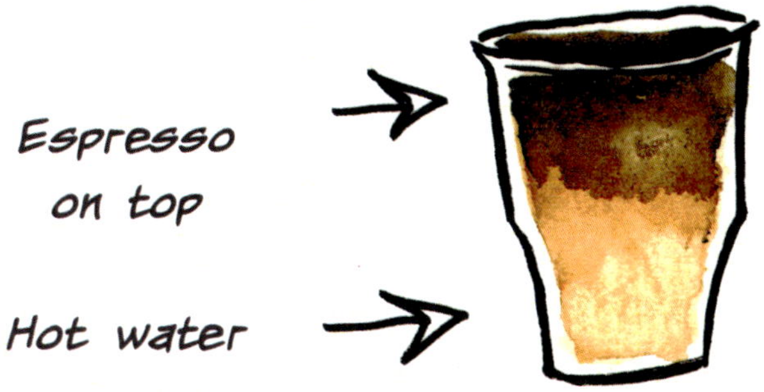

Americanos are a good alternative to drip coffee, because they are less acidic and smoother than regular coffee, and less caffeinated.

Other Steamed Milk drinks

Piccolo Latte

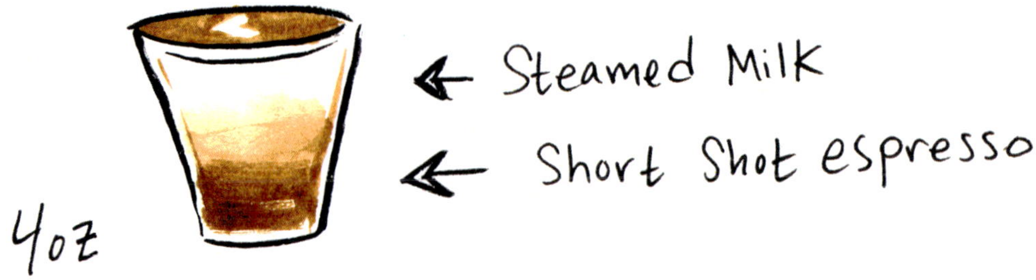

A "baby" latte, more milk then a macchiato, in theory it should have a ***ristretta*** or short shot of espresso so there is less water in the shot.

Cortado

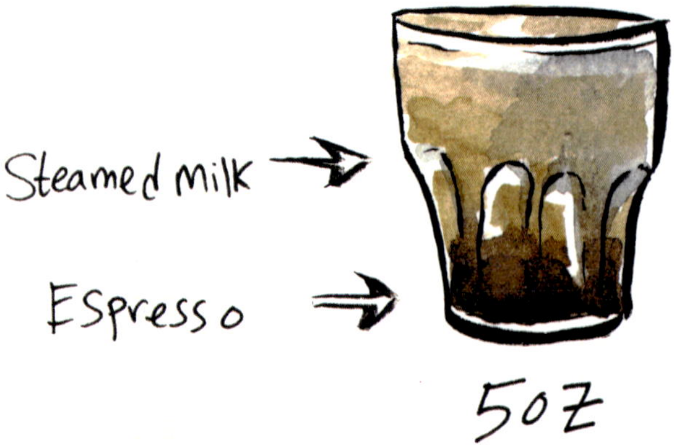

It's very close to being a ***Gibraltar*** or a piccolo latte, as well as several other countries variants. Spanish in origin and should be served in a clear glass, it also has very little milk in it.

Flat White

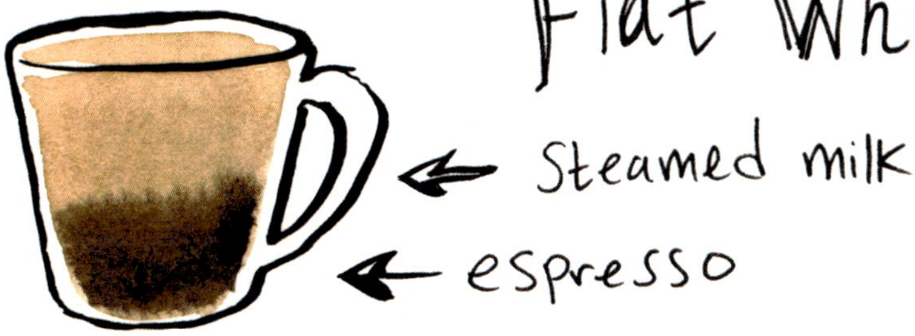

5oz

The main difference is between its other less milk brothers is there is supposed to be **very little** foam on it.

Mezzo

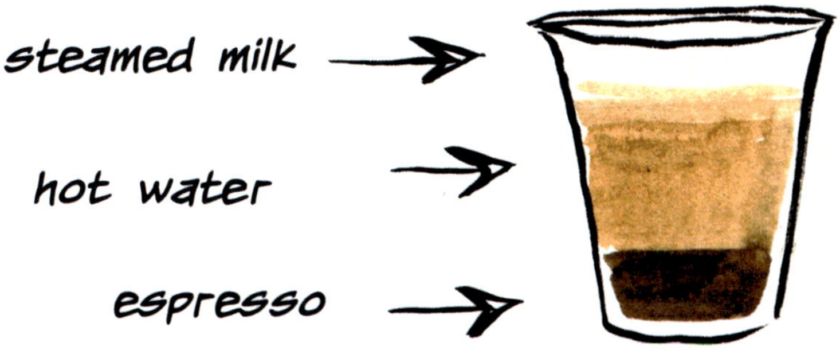

10oz - 12oz

Essentially an Americano topped with some steamed milk, like a smoother less milky Cafe au lait.

Cafe Au Lait

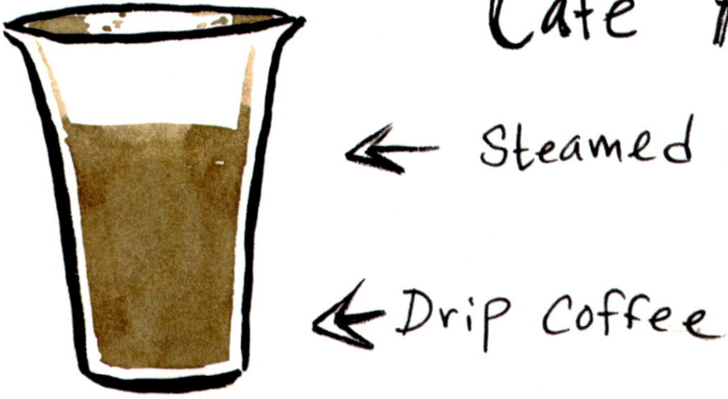

10oz - 24oz

Occasionally known as a "**Misto**" 2/3rds coffee to milk.

French Style

France has variants of the kind of coffee and espresso drinks you usually see in the U.S., though most American cafes serve Italian style drinks.

Coffee to go? Not in France. Many French cafe's don't offer a "to go" option.

Café Crème

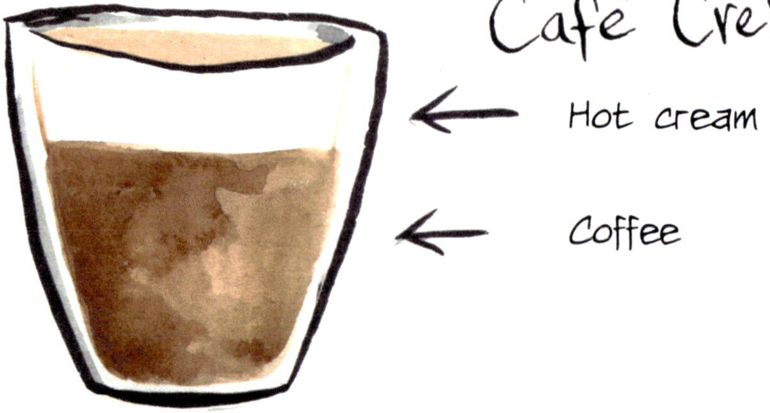

Instead of an 'au lait' this what you will find most often, 'au laits' are more popular with Americans.

Café Noisette

(Hazelnut coffee)

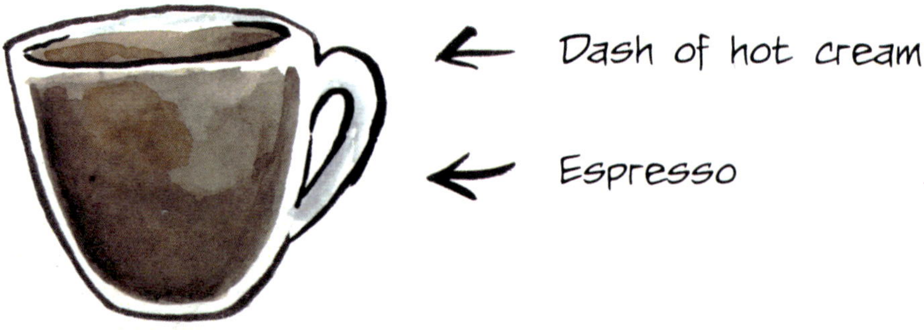

There is no hazelnut in it, the name references the color of the espresso.

*Café = **coffee**

Café Léger

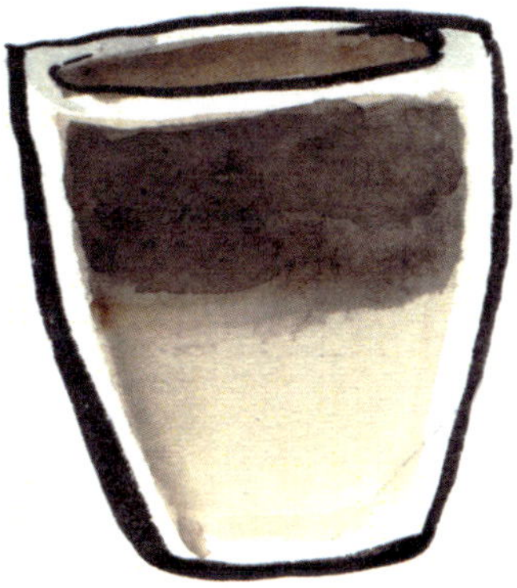

Espresso
Hot water x 2

Also known as a 'café allongé'
Like a short Americano, some times the water is served on the side so you can dilute it yourself.

Café

Strong black coffee like espresso or a French roast.

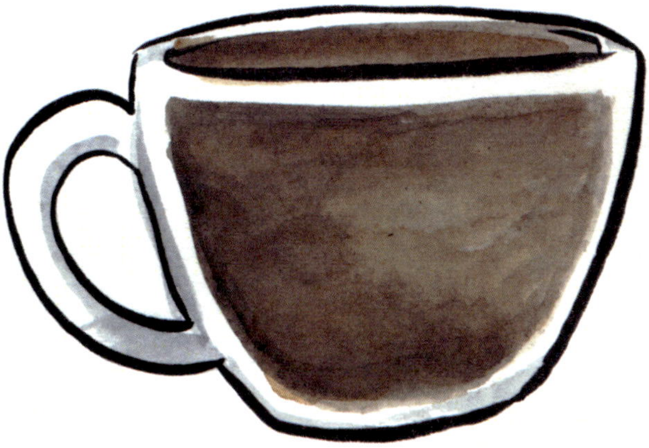

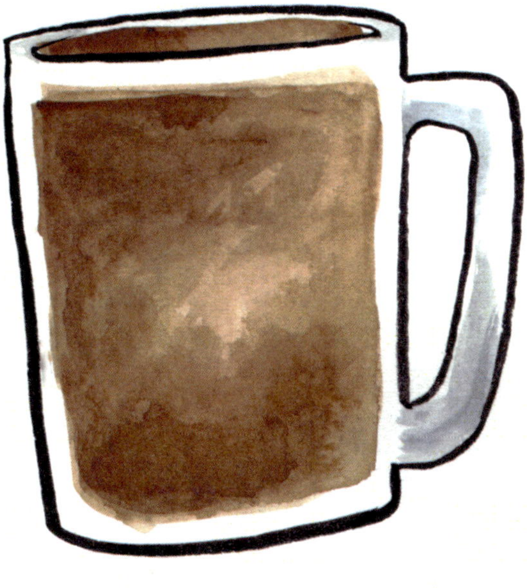

Café Americain

Filtered coffee*

Similar, to the standard American drip. Or depending on where you order it you might get an Americano. It is less strong then a 'Café'.

*'Flitered' coffee seems less common in France, most coffee is probably french press or stove top brewed, instead of auto-drip.

The Myth of the iced Cappuccino

(hint its not real)

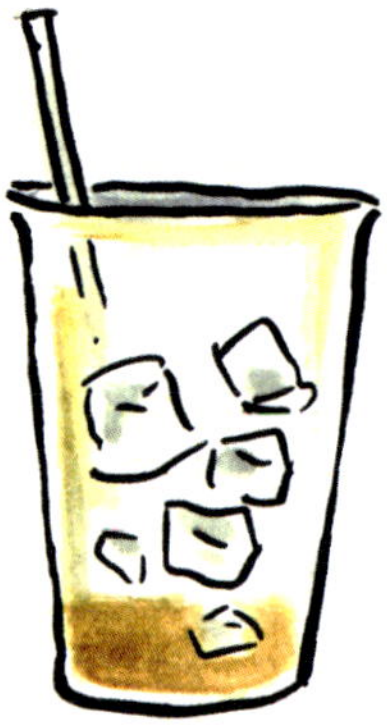

"What is it?"

Iced cappuccino are actually ***iced Lattes***

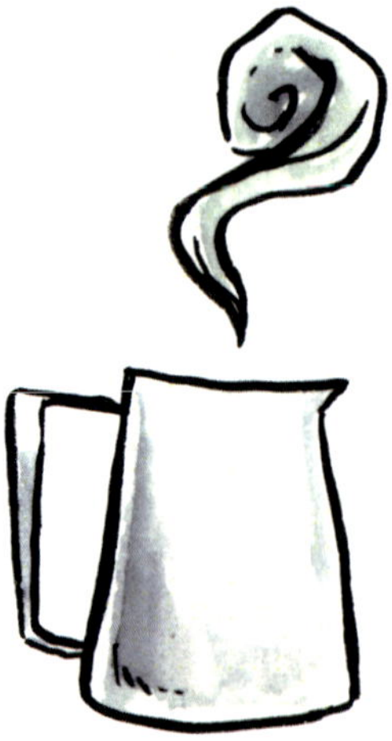

Espresso & cold milk over ice.

Unless what you wanted was steamed milk with espresso served over ice.

12 oz

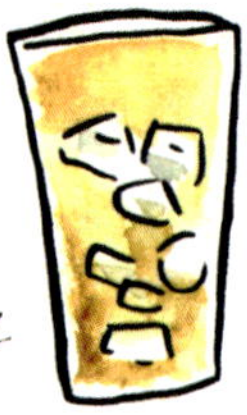

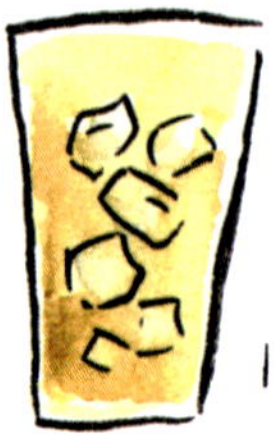

16 oz

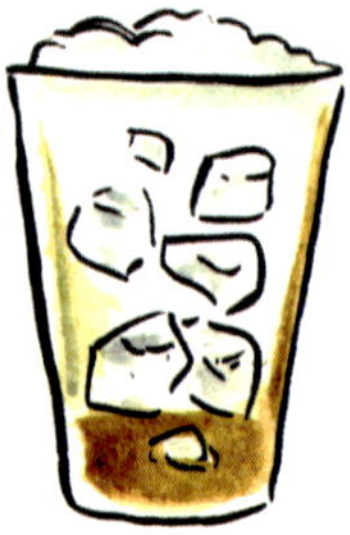

Some places serve an iced cappuccino as a small iced latte but it's still the same thing.

Over ice

Cold brew Coffee Vs. Ice brewed Coffee

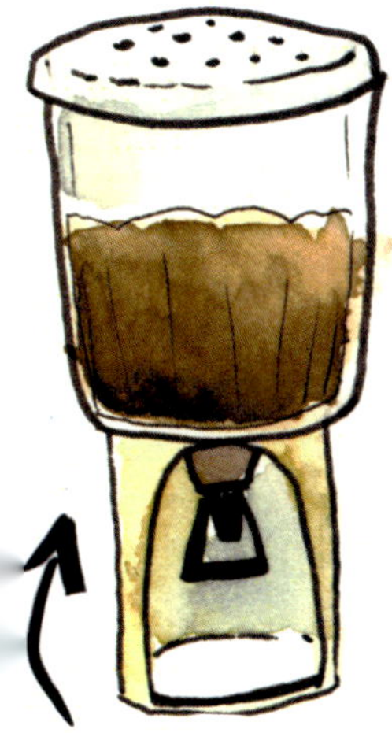

To make **Cold Brew,** the coffee grinds are soaked for **12 hours** in cold water.

5lbs of coffee to 3 gallons of water. It has the same amount of caffeine as drip coffee.

a double filter drum.

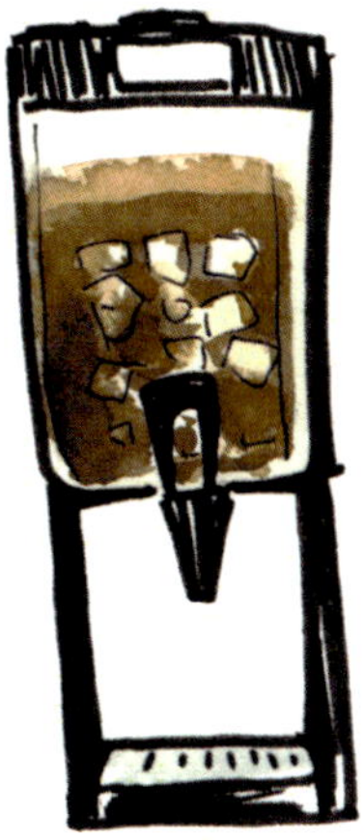

Over ice/Iced coffee

Use double the amount of coffee to hot wate,r brew the coffee over ice

Has two times as much caffeine as drip coffee.

The **cold brew** process does not fully extract the flavor of the coffee bean, which makes it smoother and less acidic than the very strong **ice brewed coffee.**

Not all coffee tastes great as cold brew.
The concentrate that **cold brew** makes is called "**toddy**" it has a **month shelf life**, toddy should be cut with equal parts water before drinking. Once you cut it it's good for a **week**.

Ice brew coffee is stale with in 24hrs.

Iced Americano

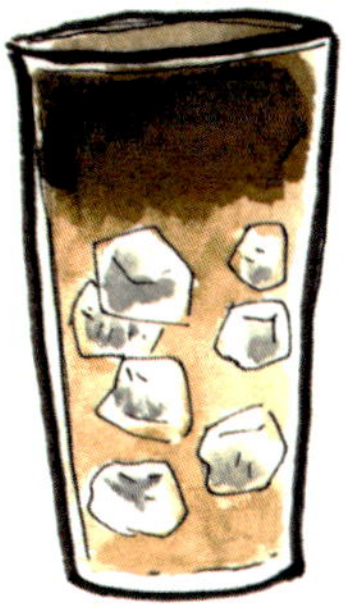

Espresso

Cold water & ice

Less acidic and less caffeine than ice brewed coffee.

Iced Latte

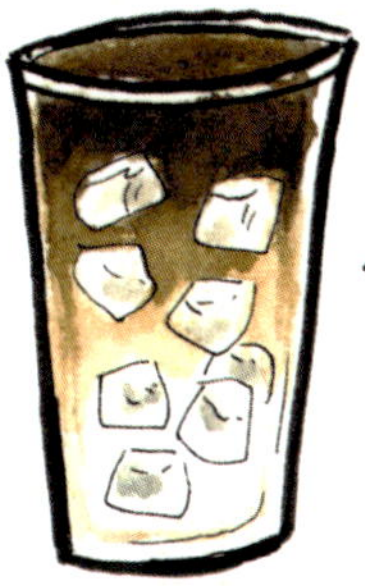

Espresso

cold milk & ice

More milky and less strong

How to brew Coffee at home

Pour over

French press

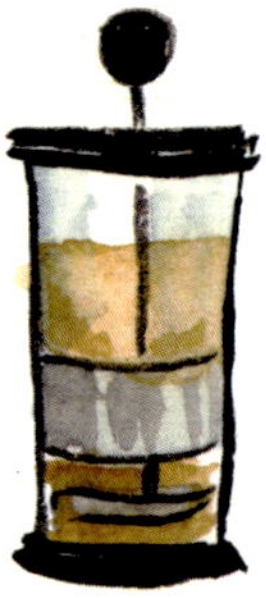

Water is added directly to the grinds. The plunger presses down the coffee grounds, and traps the grinds so you can decant the coffee. It makes for very rich coffee with a fine layer of sediment.

Chemex

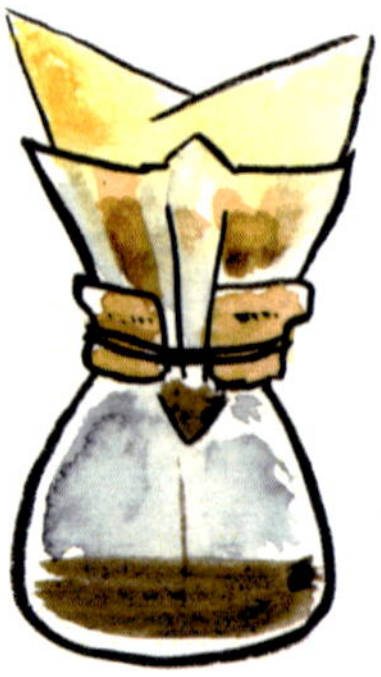

An older way to make coffee which uses a special thick filter that allows the coffee to slowly brew and drip down.

Pour over coffee uses cone filters and the hot water which is boiled ***separately*** and is poured on top of the grinds.

Hario drip

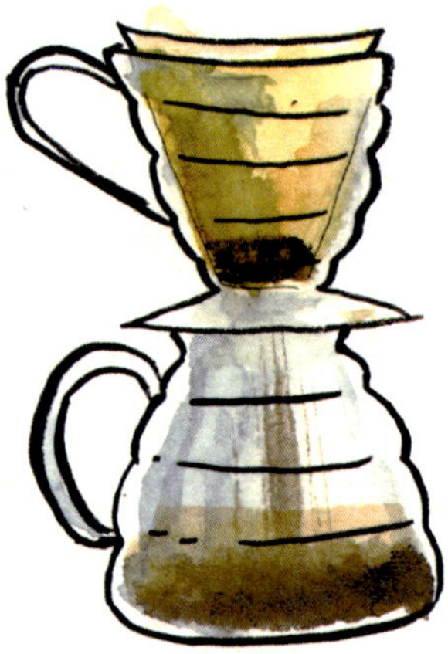

Coffee slowly drips through holes in the bottom of the dripper.

Clever drip

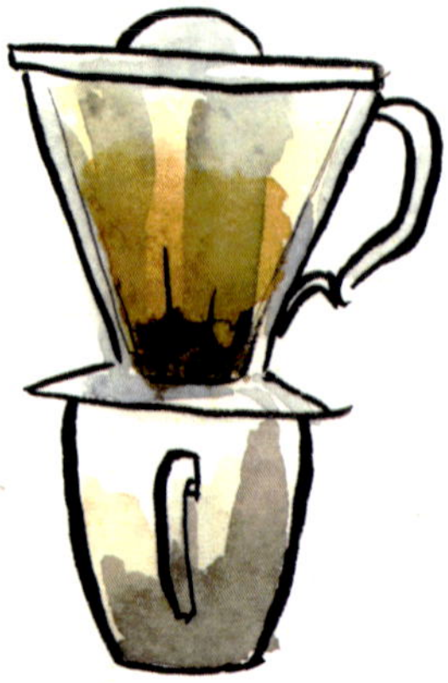

Variant of the Hario, coffee brews for 4 minutes then you release into the coffee cup after set on the cup rim.

Electric Methods

All electric coffee brewers cause a slight burning of the coffee due to water heat.

Auto-Drip methods usually called **Drip coffee**

Bottom burner coffee maker

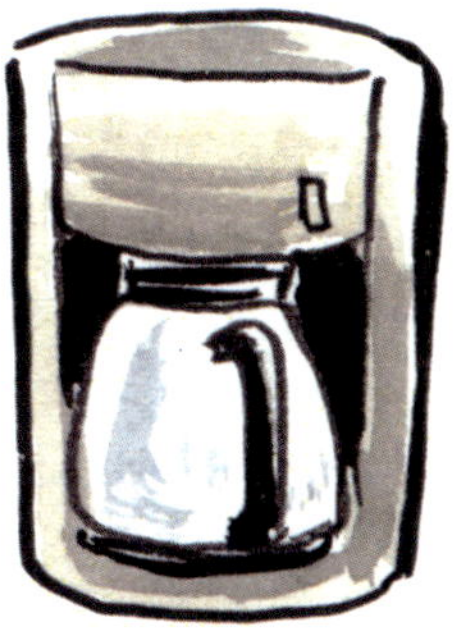

The glass carafe and liquid inside is kept heated by the burner after coffee brews. This slowly burns the coffee, and results in that end of the pot 'horror brew.'

Steel carafe auto drip

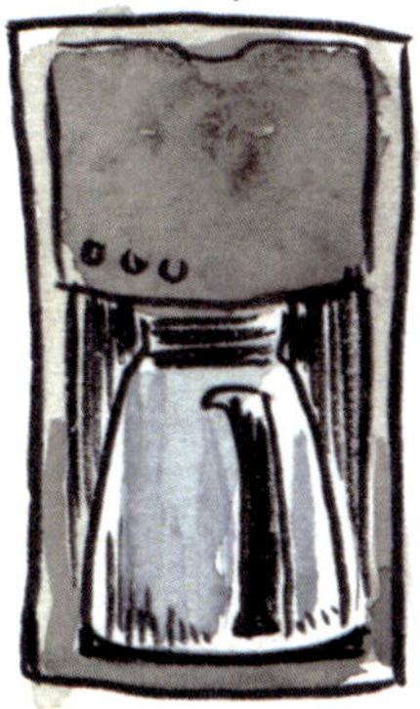

The insulated carafe keeps the coffee warm, instead of having a constant heat source. It's a more modern coffee-maker, and is the kind I recommend for people who want an Auto-drip.

Stove top espresso

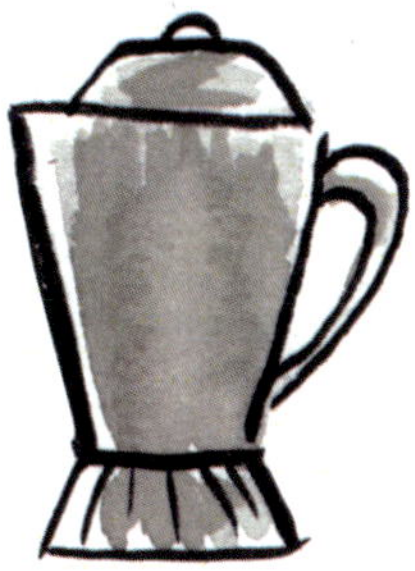

Differs from cafe espresso because it doesn't have "crema". Pressure from heat creates the force that pushes the fine ground coffee into the serving chamber.

Percolator

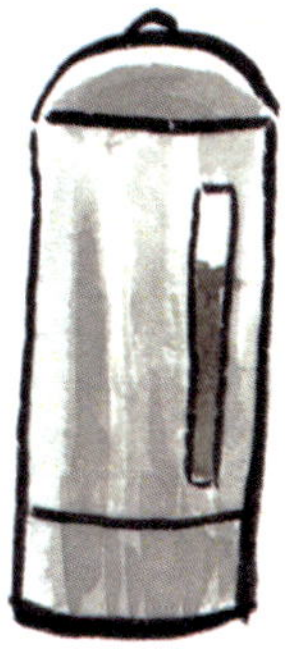

It forces boiling water through grinds into a separate chamber and cycles it through. Its brew is less flavorful and hotter than drip coffee.

Filters

Knowing what kind of filter you need for your coffee maker determines what grind/fineness to get your coffee ground to. Whether you are grinding it yourself or getting a barista to do it, knowing this is important.

Flat bottomed

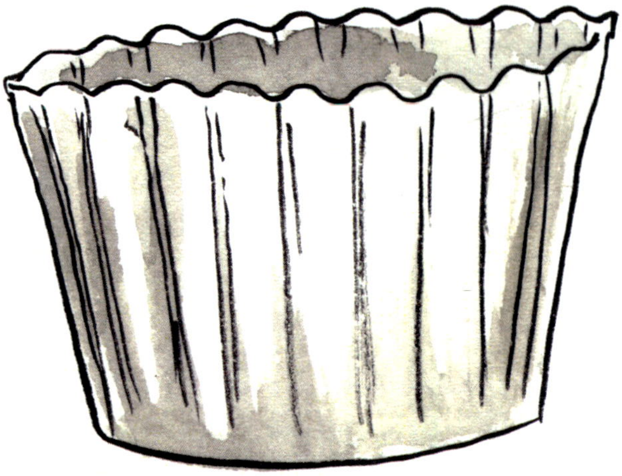

Cone

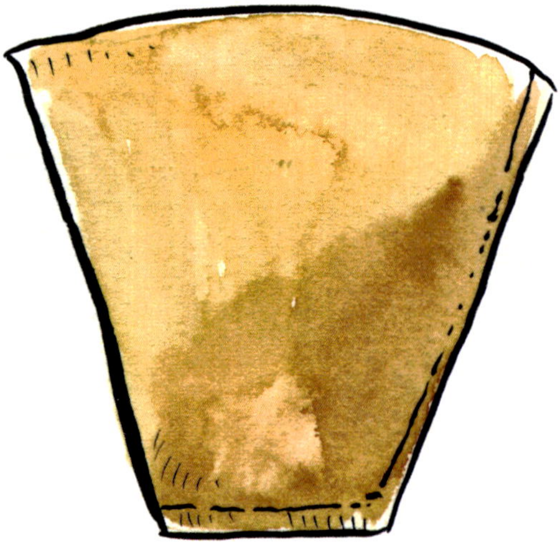

Grind: Medium

These are used only in ***drip coffee makers*** or cold brew drums. They are commonly used in industrial cafe coffee makers, and come large enough to hold 5lbs of ground coffee! They are easier to tear when wet because of the wide design, so they should be handled with care.

Grind: Fine to Medium

Used with pour-overs and many of the more recently made drip coffee brewers, these filters have slanted sides and a flat bottom. They are often referred to as a #4 filter.

Gold

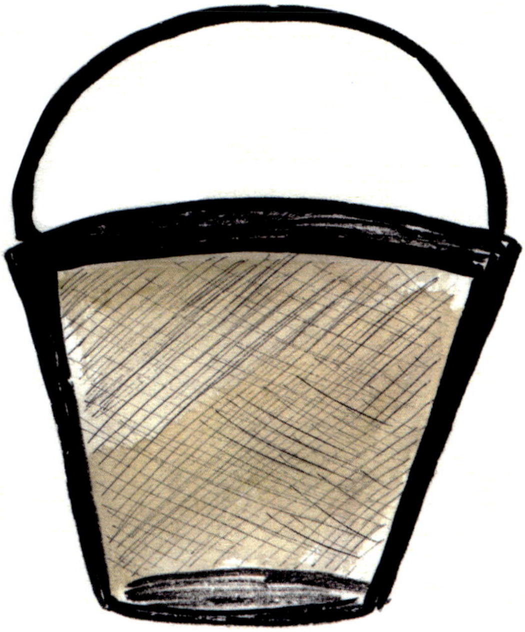

Chemex

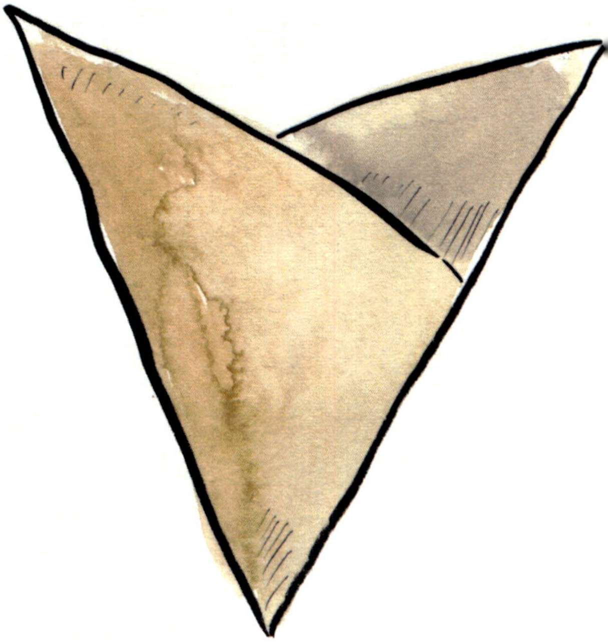

Grind: Medium

This reusable god mesh filter can be used in just about any machine or pour over. It uses paper filters comes in cone or flat bottom size. It also makes the coffee a little richer because of the extra coffee dust and lets in more of the oils that the paper filters absorb. It will leave a layer of sediment and coffee sludge on the bottom of your cup similar to a french press.

Grind: Medium to coarse

These are special Chemex only filters. They come pre-folded, or you can buy ones that you fold yourself. The coffee slowly drips through the tip of the filter, which is wedged into the neck of the Chemex. This filter is a thicker paper than the other paper filters.

Know your grind!

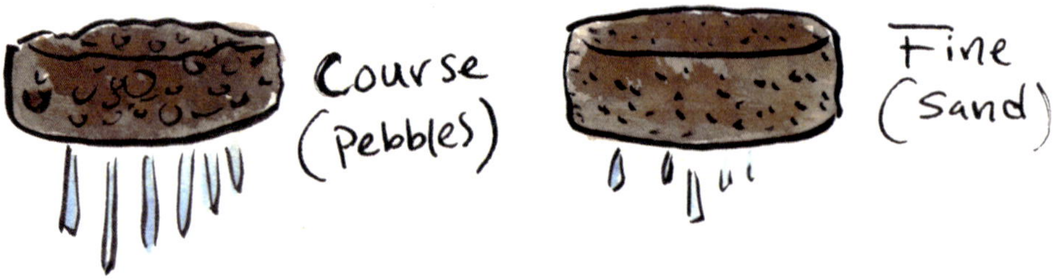

Water is lazy and moves more easily through course ground then fine ground.

Following up on filter and filter-less **know your grind**

Espresso/Cappuccino machines: extra fine grind
Auto-Drip coffeemakers using paper filters: fine-medium grind
Auto-Drip coffeemakers with metal-mesh filter: medium grind
pour-over: Medium-coarse grind
Pour-over with cone filter: Fine-Medium grind
Chemex: Coarse grind
French Press: coarse grind
Percolator: coarse grind

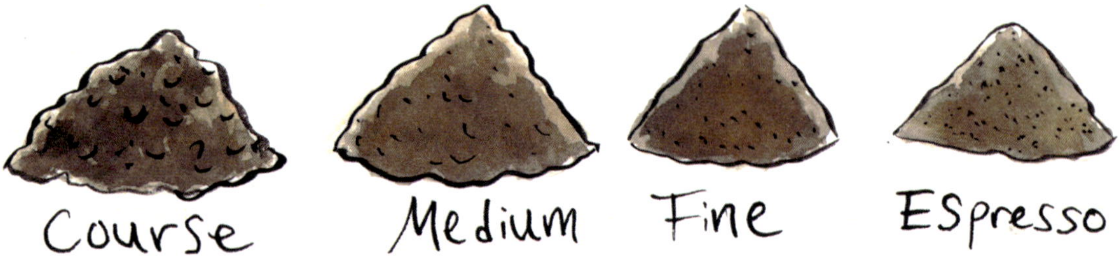

Coffee Grinders At Home

Burr

Burr grinders evenly grind beans by crushing them. They have adjustable settings, so you can easily switch between grinds. This means if you have more than one coffee making method, you can change without hassle. There are many cost effective home electric versions on the market now.

Blade

Blade grinders chop and cut up beans like a food processor. The results are uneven sized chunks, which make for less balanced brews. If you are using a blade grinder, make sure to grind in pulses, and don't grind too much at once.

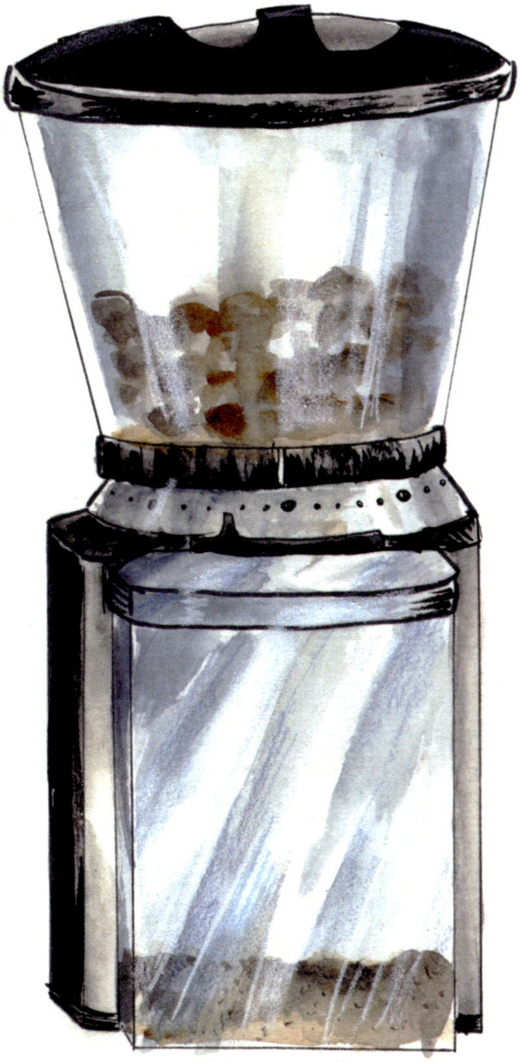

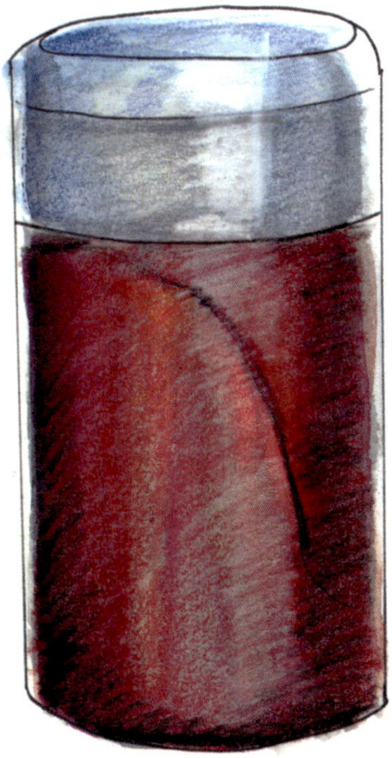

It is important to clean your grinders, as they build up a film of old coffee oil and grinds. Make sure to dry wipe them down on a regular basis. You can grind white rice in your burr grinders to help clean out the oils as well.

Water Saturation in brewing methods

How much of the water comes in contact with the grounds also affects the balance of the brew flavor, like how bitter or smooth it is.

Automatic Electric Drip Coffee Makers

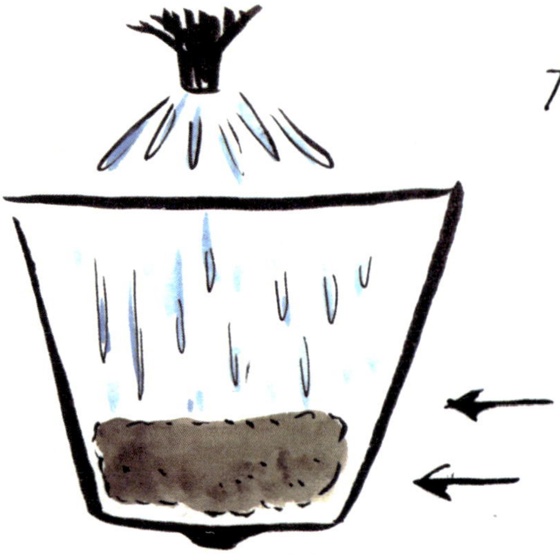

Water in the auto-drip rains down and has to soak through the top of the grinds, to "drip" into the pot. This uneven distribution of saturation leads to an uneven extraction, which is an issue with most auto-drip machines.

Brew tip: One way to help negate this issue is to open up the lid mid brew and give the coffee grinds a stir.

In NYC we have good tap water, but if you live in an area with bad tap water (i.e. hard water) you should brew with filtered water or spring water. This can affect the flavor of the coffee.

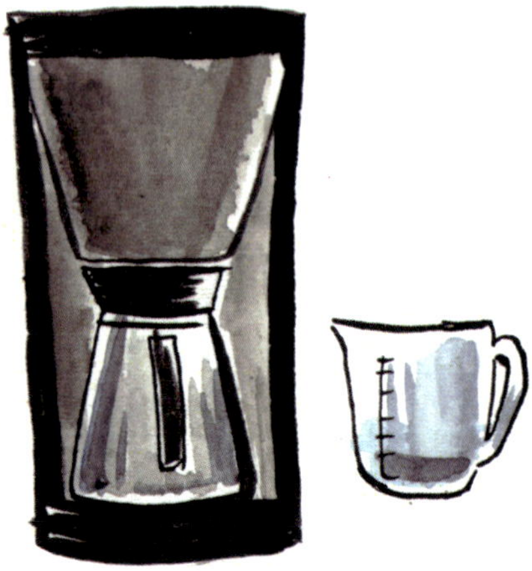

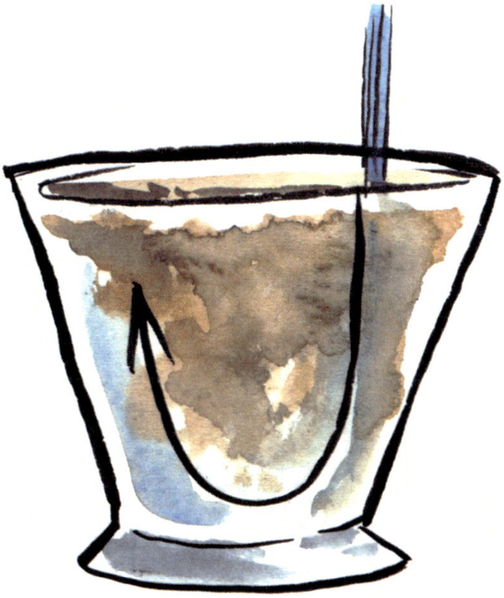

The water in 'Pour Over' and 'French Presses' forces its way under the grinds and allows for even more water coverage.

Tips for proper pour over brewing

1) When pouring the water, do so slowly and in a spiraling motion, until you fully cover the grinds with just a little water

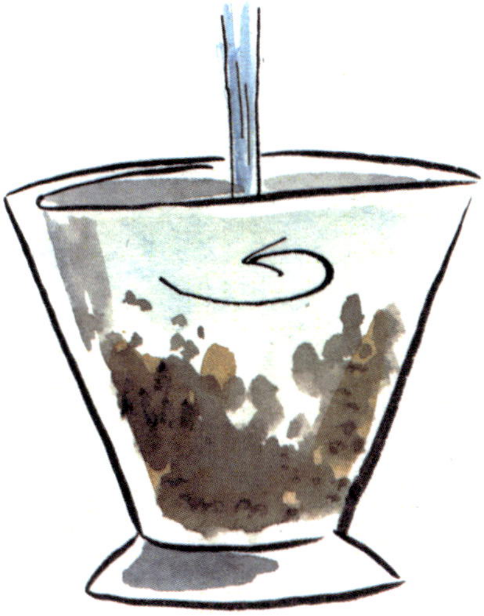

2) Wait about 30 seconds for the dome of the "bloom," which is the initial puffing of the wet grinds, to fall

3) Continue to pour water

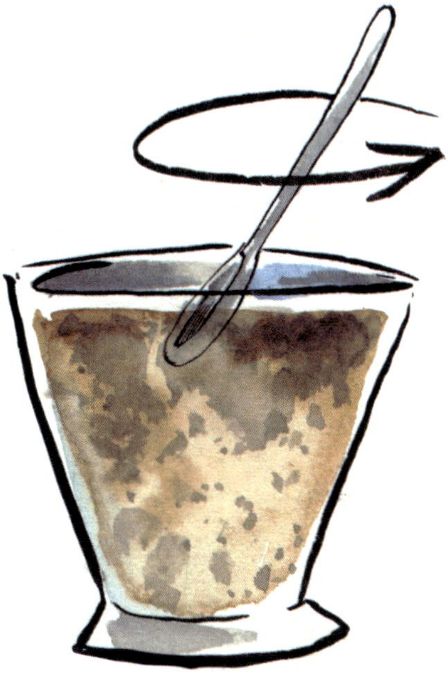

4) Use a spoon to gently stir the water and grinds.

5) If using a timed pour over like a "clever drip" or French Press, wait 3 minutes and then stir, then wait one more minute before serving.

Brewing at home

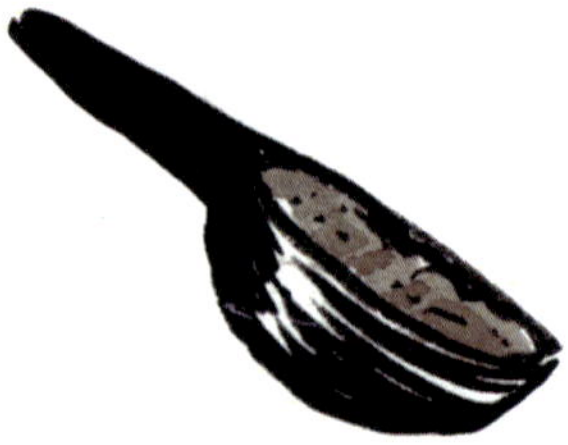

Ratios:

Auto-drip:

1 scoop of coffee to 6 -8 oz of water.
So 1-2 scoops to 1 cup

French press/pour over: 4 scoops to 12oz.
Each Scoop is 2 table spoons

If you find the pot of coffee gets ***progressively*** worse as you drink it, you may be using ***too much*** coffee to ***not enough*** water. If you like strong coffee, you are better off just getting a stronger roast coffee instead of just over-saturating a pot.

French Press & Clever drips

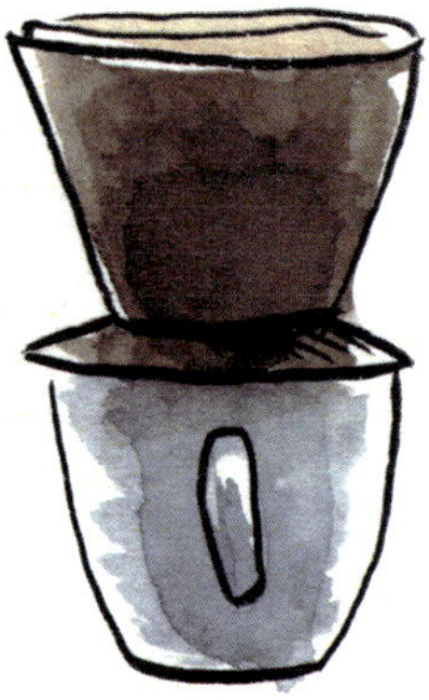

Any press or drip system that ***requires*** you to time it needs ***4 minutes to brew***. Set a timer, ***over*** brewing also burns coffee! Make sure the water is boiling tempature, ***2 minutes*** in a microwave, or use a tea kettle.

Some important notes:

Storage:

Keep your coffee in an ***airtight bag*** or container ***at room temperature***. ***Do not*** store close to a heat source, because over time the beans will slowly burn and become ruined. ***Do not*** store in the ***fridge*** or ***freezer***. The coffee will lose its smell, which is an important part to the flavor when you brew it.

Patience:

It is better if you ***wait*** till the ***coffee is done*** brewing before pouring your first cup, because the weaker coffee at the start balances the darker brew near the end of drip process.

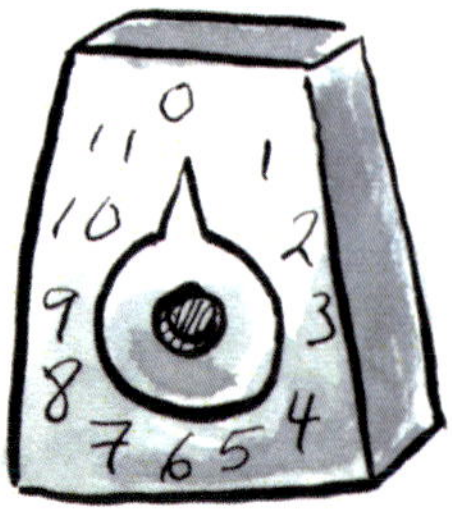

How does Coffee get burned?

Here are some common ways coffee gets burned/damaged.

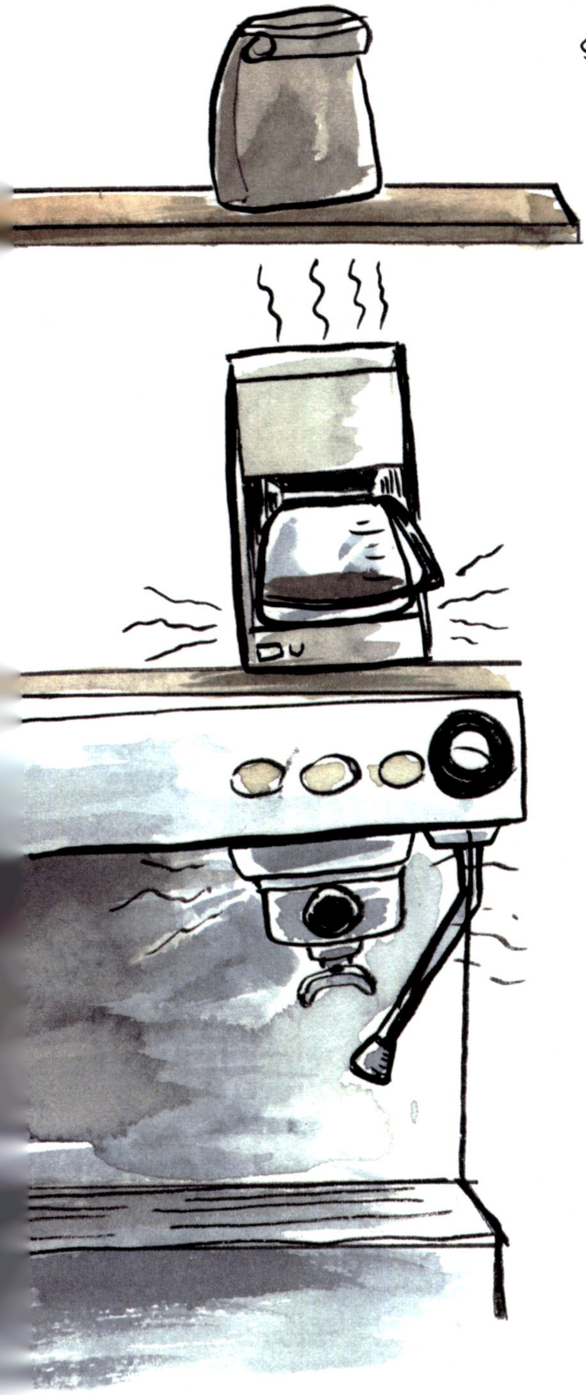

1) Storing coffee beans above a heat source like an oven, a coffee maker or other machinery that gives off heat.

2) Coffee makers with **bottom burners**; the heat slowly boils it down and the coffee burns.

3) If the barista waits too long before running a shot of espresso after they lock the prepped porta-filter into the espresso maker.

New Orleans Style

New Orleans is a blend that shows up in some shops. It's a coffee blend that can be drunk cold or hot, and is recommended with cream because it uses dark roast coffee and is very strong when drunk black. Usually the blend is up to 30% chicory and 70% coffee, so it is less caffeinated than straight up coffee.

Back in the day when coffee was even more of a luxury, and everything had to travel by boat, chicory was used as an additive to stretch out coffee supplies. It is also considered a flavor additive.

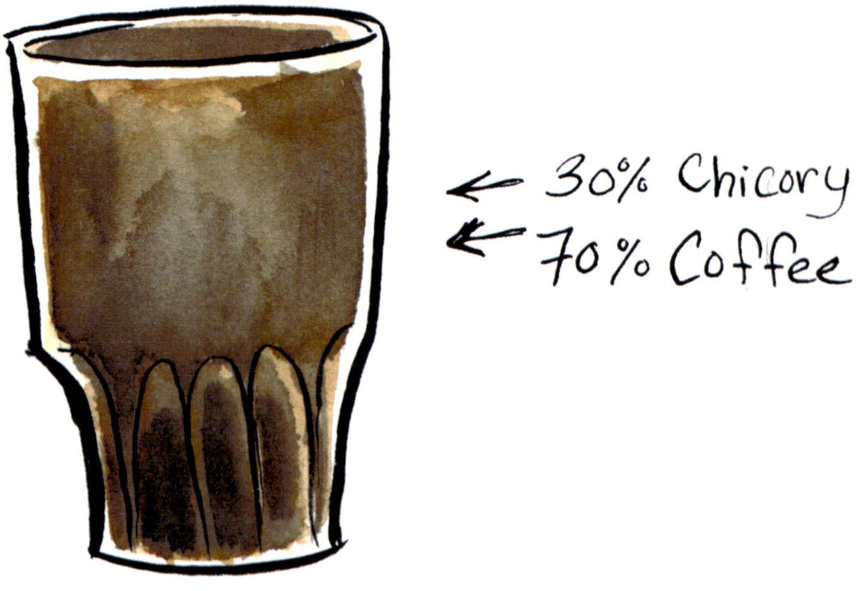

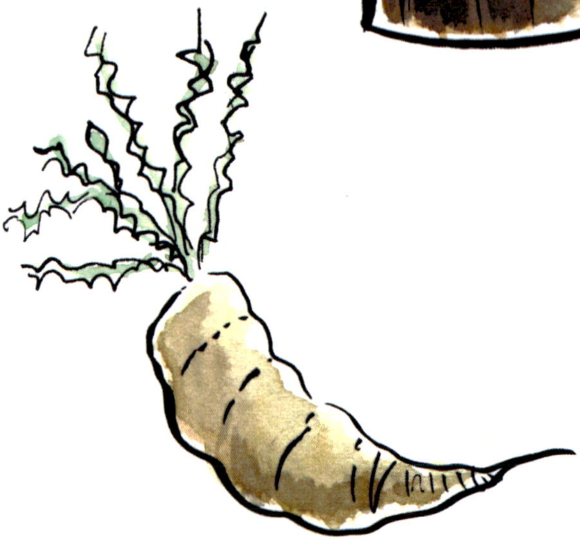

Chicory is a flowering plant, the root of which has a strong flavor. It has been used as a coffee substitute and additive, it's caffeine free

Decaf Coffee beans

How **do** you get the **caffeine** out of the **bean**?

It is impossible to actually remove ***all*** the caffeine from coffee, so even "decaf" is actually slightly caffeinated. All of the processes used to remove caffeine from the beans change the natural robust flavor and smell of coffee. The caffeine removal process is done with green coffee beans, before they are roasted.

Swiss Water process

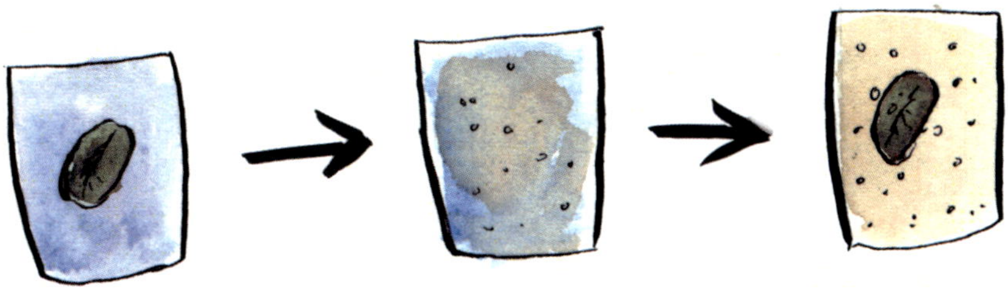

Currently the industry preferred method of decaffeination, because it is less chemical then the other processes.

Unroasted coffee is soaked in water to remove the caffeine, though the process also removes most of the flavor. The caffeinated water is then treated to separate the flavor from the caffeine, and then the beans are soaked once more to re-infuse the flavor back in. Once the beans dry they are then roasted and ready to be brewed.

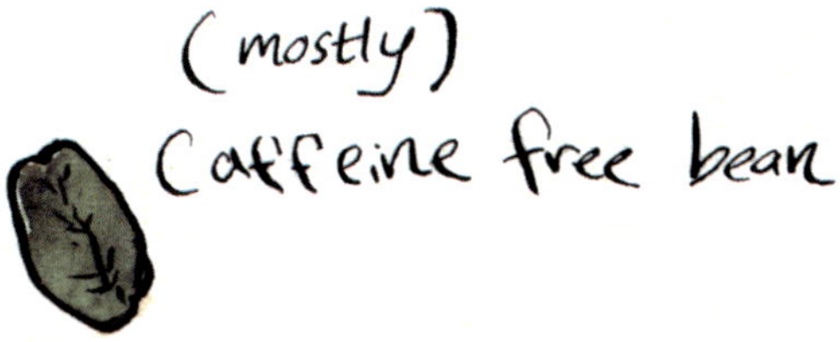

CO_2 Process

Green coffee beans are soaked in compressed carbon dioxide, which removes the caffeine from the coffee. The CO_2 is then filtered using an activated carbon filter to extract the caffeine so the CO_2 can later be reused to remove more caffeine from the coffee..

Sparkling Water Process

CO_2 is used here as well, but the CO_2 has the caffeine washed from it using sparkling water in a secondary tank, which is recycled to remove more caffeine from the beans.

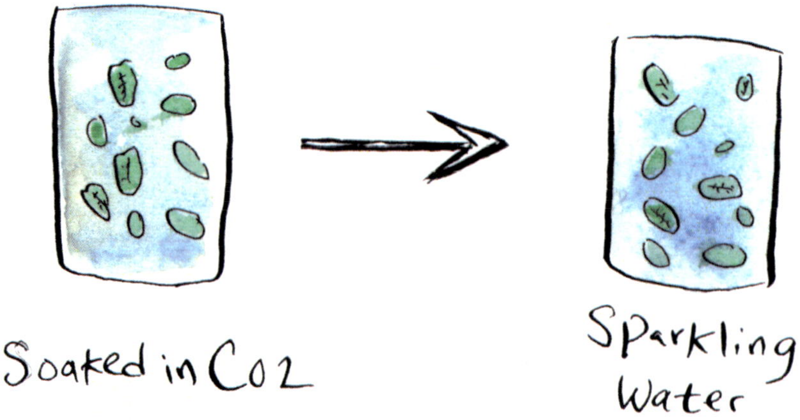

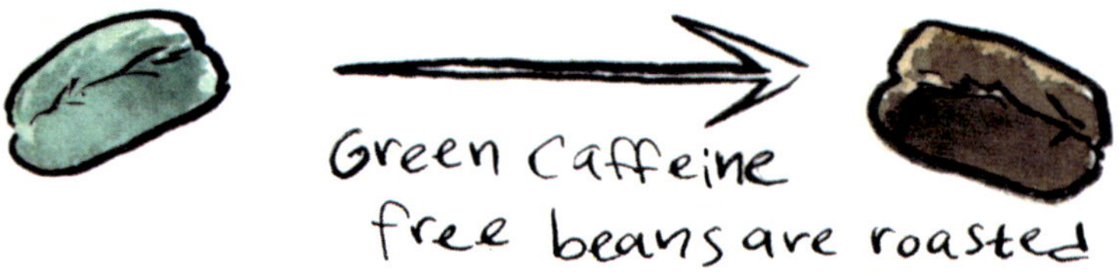

It's NOT Coffee

Chai Latte

Chai is a mix of black tea & various spices. Chai means "Tea" so "chai tea" its redundant. The Chai Latte is made a few different ways, but no, ***it is not coffee.***

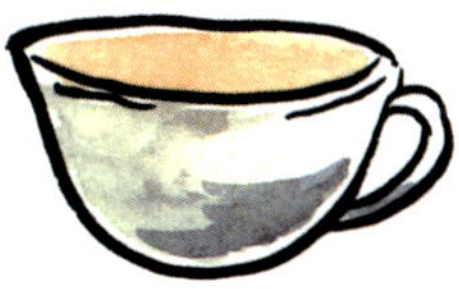

Chai Concentrate

Liquid chai combined with milk & then steamed; usually pre-sweetened.

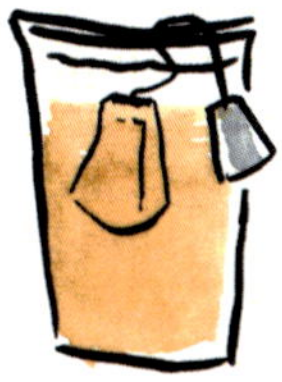

Poormans Chai

Bagged chai, which is brewed with hot water & ***topped*** with steamed milk.

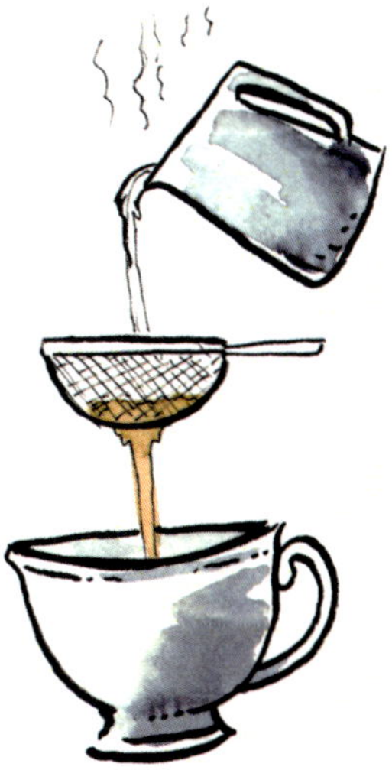

Powder Chai

Fine ground chai with the hot water poured through it to make a strong shot of tea finished with steamed milk.

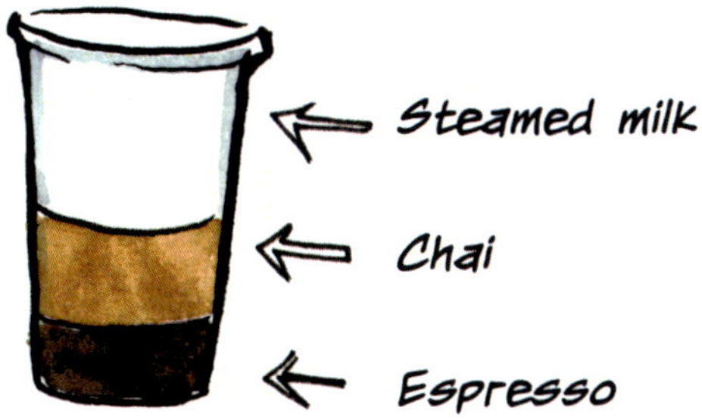

Dirty Chai

A chai latte made with a shot of ***espresso*** added.

Matcha Latte

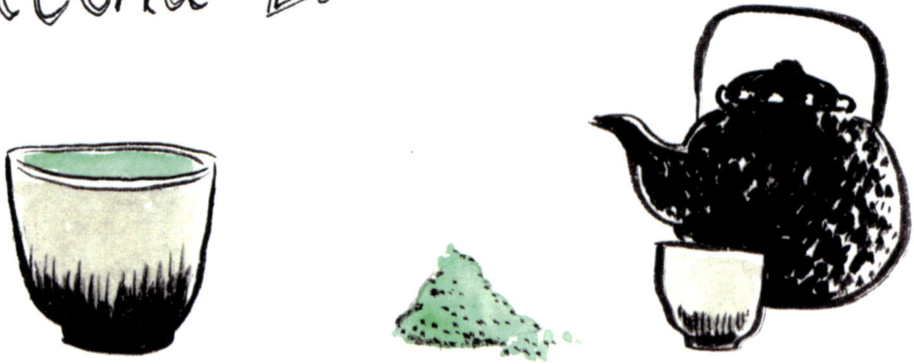

Matcha is ground Japanese green tea, the consistency of a fine powder. It is whisked with hot water to prepare, and is most often used in tea ceremonies.

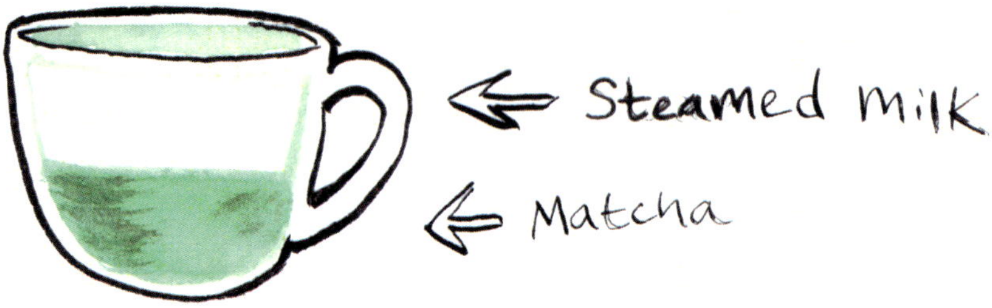

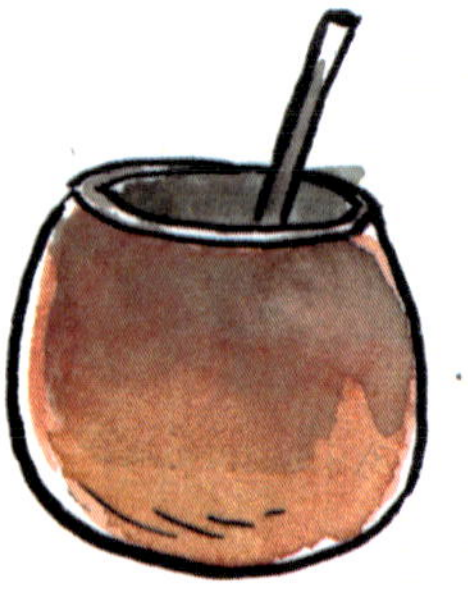

Yerba Mate

Yerba Mate is an herbal tea that has natural stimulants that have a similar effect to caffeine. It is drunk out of a hollow gourd with a metal straw. It has become a popular cafe drink in the last couple of years. You can re-brew it by adding more hot water and loose tea floats at the top. It is not supposed to be stirred, but steeped.

Weird Coffee facts

Two of the world's most expensive coffee beans are collected by animals, which also double as quality control picking, and cherry processing.

Civet Coffee aka Kopi luwak

Found in Indonesia, civets are cat and weasel like animals who eat the coffee cherries for the fruit. After being eaten, the coffee beans are ultimately passed through their digestive tract and then harvested from the Civets poop. By harvesting the beans this way, the cherries don't have to be "**processed**," because the mammalian digestive system removes the cherry and pulp, leaving the bean.

These beans can sell for up to $160-$500 per pound, and anywhere from $30 to $90 a cup.

Some cafes that serve Civet coffee will also provide you with a certificate of authenticity

There is now a synthetically produced developed by the university of Florida that reproduces the effects the civet's digestive system. It's much cheaper than actual Civet coffee, and is processed without real animal digestion.

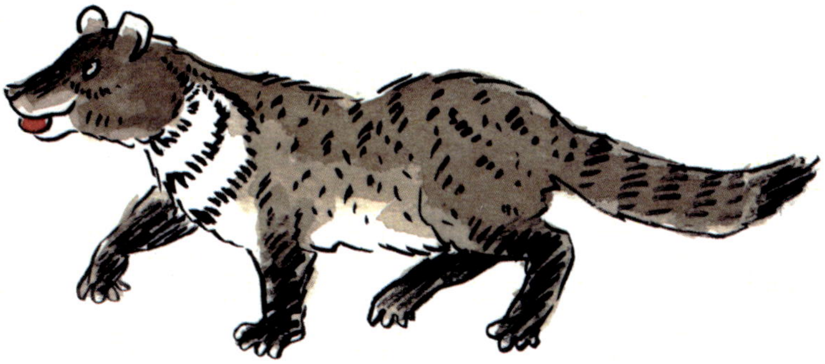

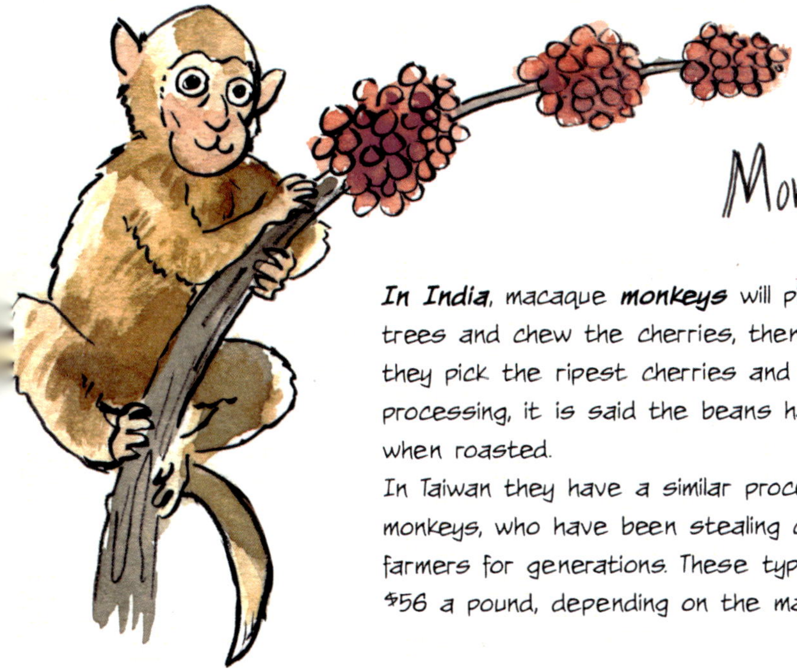

Monkey Coffee

In India, macaque ***monkeys*** will pick the coffee cherries from the trees and chew the cherries, then spit the beans out. Because they pick the ripest cherries and handle most of the fruit processing, it is said the beans have a pleasant sweet taste when roasted.

In Taiwan they have a similar process using Formosan rock monkeys, who have been stealing coffee cherries from coffee farmers for generations. These types of coffee retail for about $56 a pound, depending on the market.

Afterword:

When I began this book, I my goal was very simple: To teach people what they were ordering when they stepped up to their local café counters, and to provide a quick reference guide for those interested in coffee. I wanted to collect all that I knew from my experi4ences as a barista in one place so that people would be prepared when it came time to get their delicious caffeinated drinks. While making this book, however, I found I learned more about art and technicalities of making and drinking coffee than I started out knowing. I have had to go examine every part of the subject I wanted to explain and then do additional research.

If you ever had a moment at a cafe where you thought: "**What's so hard about making my drink,"** or " **geez why is this taking so long??"** I hope reading this book will give you some insight into how much work goes into making good coffee.

Every cafe and roaster has a slightly different method or variation for how certain drinks are prepared and the sizes of the cups that are used. I say this to explain that there is no one correct way, and that every cafe is different. It is also important to say that barista training is primarily through hands on experience and verbal explanation and correction.

This was the most frustrating thing in the book writing process, knowing that there is no way to be 100% correct in explaining the processes but wanting to write anyway.

I've been a professional barista for 5 years, its helped fund my indie comic book printings and my vices, coffee being chief among them. I recently retired as a barista for a carreer job in animation, so this is my lovenote to coffee culture, as I'm only a consumer now. It's bitter sweet, but my love for fine coffee will always be true.

Thanks to my first manager Queenie for being a hard ass with high standards, to my shop Dépanneur in Brooklyn for letting me sass customers and having the coolest co-workers. Thanks to the coffee Roasters, Counter Culture and Intelligentsia for teaching me about coffee.

Vita, my fine pro bono editor who had to keep telling me to better explain things for the less coffee geekish. And dealt wiith my very bad grammar and spelling like a saint.

Also to Pat, BB & Vita for bullying me into finally doing this book.

Cheers yeah!?

-SW

APPENDIX I
GLOSSARY

Aerating - the process of introducing air into milk to create foam

Auto-Drip maker: Electric coffee maker that sprays water over ground coffee and brews into a pot.

Barista - The Italian word for bartender, used to describe a coffee counter person

Basket see **Porta-filter**

Blends - A selection of different coffee beans E.I: House blend

Body - strong flavor of the coffee or espresso

Bright - a flavor note used to describe a acidic or citrus coffee

Burr grinder - A special coffee grinder used for espresso for grinding per shot

Clean finish - Describing a good shot of espresso, leaves no sour aftertaste in your mouth

Coffee Cherry - the fruit coffee beans are harvested from, they are edible.

Cold brew - coffee that has soaked in cold water for 24hrs to brew

Crema - as the shot finishes, the espresso thins and forms a golden foam.

Dosing - The act of grinding espresso into the port a-filter using a burr grinder

Drip coffee - see *Auto-drip*

Fair trade - Certifying the coffee was harvested from democratically-organized cooperatives of small producers, not individually-owned farms, estates, or farms that use hired labor.

Filters - What is used to prevent grinds from ending up in espresso or coffee

Flavor notes - or *Tasting notes*. Coffee has complex flavors beyond coffee, different beans have different flavor notes like wine does. Most fine coffee lists the tasting notes on the bag.

Foam - the body or head of the steamed milk used in drinks

Half caf - ½ normal coffee ½ decaf

Hulling - is like shelling for coffee beans, its when you remove the dried left over skin around the bean.

APPENDIX I
GLOSSARY

Iced Coffee - Strong coffee brewed using a coffee maker over ice

Leveling - using your fingers to smooth out the espresso grounds before it can be tamped

Long black - Reverse Americano

Port a-filter - The metal filter that fits into the basket on espresso makers

Pulling - Term for brewing a shot of espresso
Pour over - Coffee brew method for brewing single cups of coffee slowly

Puck - an disk of packed wet espresso grinds after the shot has been pulled

Region - Place of origin where coffee cherries were harvested

Roast - The length of time the beans have been cooked for

Roaster - The company that roasts the green coffee beans

Running - see pulling, the action of brewing espresso. ex. running a shot

Shot - A single or double shot of espresso

Single origin - A batch of coffee that has been harvested from one place

Sinking - Part of milk steaming that raises milk temperature

Steamed milk - Milk that has hot air forced into it to raise the temperature and aerated it for drinks

Steam wand - the part of the espresso machine used to steam milk

Stretching - see "sinking"

Surfing - Part of milking steaming that introduces air.

Tamping - the act of packing ground espresso into a port-a-filter so it can be run

APPENDIX II

My favorite NYC coffee shops

Depanneur
North 3rd and Wythe ave, williamsburg Brooklyn
Serves: Intelligentsia

The West Tavern
379 Union Ave
Williamsburg, Brooklyn
Serves: Brooklyn Roasting company

Blue Bottle
160 Berry St, N5th
Williamsburg, Brooklyn
Serves: Blue Bottle

Everyman Espresso
13th Street, bet. 3rd and 4th ave
Union Square, Manhattan
Serves: Counter Culture Coffee

Third Rail coffee
240 Sullivan St
(between Bleecker St & 3rd St)
Greenwich Village, Manhattan
Serves: Counter Culture Coffee

Cafe Grumpy
224 West 20th Street
Chelsea, Manhattan
(Has more than one location)
Serves: Cafe Grumpy

Stumpton
Ace Hotel
20 West 29th st at broadway
Serves: Stumptown

The art of Joe
Many Locations
(Mid-town, East village, West village)
Serves: Art of Joe

Toby's estate
125 N 6th St
(between Berry St & Bedford Ave)
Williamsburg. Brooklyn
Serves: Toby's

Seattle

Victrola Coffee
310 E Pike St
Serves: Victrola Coffee

Monorail Espresso
520 Pike St
(between 5th Ave & 6th Ave)
Serves: ???

Washington, DC

Tryst Coffee House
2459 18th St NW
(between N Belmont Rd & N Columbia Rd)
Serves: Counter Culture Coffee

Big Bear cafe
1700 1st St NW
(between N R St & N Florida Ave)
Serves: Counter Culture Coffee

Filter Coffeehouse & Espresso bar
1726 20th St NW
(between N S St & N R St)
Serves: Ceremony Coffee

Chinatown Coffee Co.
475 H St NW
(between N 4th St & N 5th St)
Serves: Intelligentsia, plus guest roasts

SOCAL California

Klatch Coffee
806 W Arrow Hwy, Ste A
San Dimas
Serves: Klatch Coffee

Florida

Bold Bean coffee roasters
869 Stockton Street #1
Jacksonville

APPENDIX IV
Some Resources

Get your coffee nerd on at these sites

http://coffeegeek.com
http://baristabrothers.com
http://www.coffeescience.org/
http://home-barista.com
http://www.sweetmarias.com/ - Coffee supplies, maker my favorite pour over brewer, plus articles on home roasting.

"**Everything but Espresso**" by Scott Rao
http://www.professionalbaristashandbook.com/

"The perfect cappuccino" (Documentary)
http://www.cappuccinomovie.com/